My Prayer Book

My Prayer Book

COMPILED BY
MICHAEL HOLLINGS

McCrimmons
Great Wakering Essex

First published in Great Britain in 1997 by
McCrimmon Publishing Co Ltd
10-12 High Street, Great Wakering, Essex SS3 0EQ
Tel (01702) 218956 Fax (01702) 216082

My Prayer Book – ISBN 0 85597 556 3
(a new edition of the former *Catholic Prayer Book for Schools*)

Cum originali concordat
Nihil obstat
Imprimatur
2nd March 1977

John P. Dewis
Gordon Read, M.A., B.D.
Christopher Creede, V.G.

ACKNOWLEDGEMENTS

The grail Psalms translated from the Hebrew by the Grail, copyright © 1963, The Grail
(England) and published by William Collins and Sons Ltd in '*The Psalms: A New
Translation.*' Used by permission.

The Jerusalem Bible Version of the Scriptures, copyrighted © in 1966, 1967 and 1968 by
Darton, Longman and Todd Ltd and Doubleday and Co. Inc., and used by permission.

The Trustees of the Tagore Estate and Macmillan, London and Basingstoke, for the prayer
by Rabindranath Tagore.

Excerpts from the English translation of *Rite of Baptism for Children* ©1969, International
Committee on English in the Liturgy, Inc. (ICEL); the English translation of the Order of
Mass from *The Roman Missal* ©1973, ICEL; excerpts from the English translation of *Holy
Communion of the Eucharist outside Mass* ©1973, ICEL; excerpts from the English
translation of *Eucharistic Prayers for Masses with Children* ©1975, ICEL; excerpts from
the English translation of *Rite of Confirmation*, Second Edition ©1975, ICEL; excerpts
from the English translation of *Pastoral Care of the Sick: Rites of Anointing and Viaticum*
©1982, ICEL; excerpts from the English translation of *Order of Christian Funerals* ©1985,
ICEL. All rights reserved.

Illustrations by The Benedictine Nuns of Turvey Abbey
(available as clip art on CD for Windows and Mac OS)
Cover design: Nick Snode
Typeset in Times 10/10.5 and Isbell ITC
Printed and bound by Thanet Press Ltd., Margate, Kent

Contents

Introduction

This is a prayer book put together for use at home, in schools, in prayer groups, in groups that come together to learn about and celebrate our faith, and so on. All ages can use it, if it suits them.

You see, really life is for each of us a time and place of learning. We can and should learn all the time – from TV or radio or video; from family life, our friends and neighbours; from animals. We are constantly gaining knowledge and experience in reading, in sport, in going to clubs and discos, in a birth or a death in the family.

You see, God is ONE, and God has given us LIFE. So everything comes together in this ONE LIFE. God is LOVE, wanting us to learn love in the school of life – together. So we get together, sometimes into smaller groups of years, or friends, or houses or teams.

Prayer is getting to know God and each other. We can learn about God and each other when we pray alone, but somehow it is often easier when we pray together in groups. Prayer helps us to share prayer and some of the deeper things in us. In a group we share our thoughts and hopes, our sadness and joy. We learn from big and small groups. We can pray in song, in using ordinary familiar prayers - like the ones in this book, or making up our own. We can pray by making music ourselves with guitars or drums or keyboards, or in listening to the music others make. We can pray in quiet times or in lively times. We can feel free with the God who has made us free.

If we learn the joy of being together and praying, we can come to the assembly of church on a Sunday at Mass and bring our spirit to the bigger community of the world. You can work for the poor, for the starving in the world, for peace, for justice, for those who suffer physically or mentally. In so many ways our energy and love can be shown.

The future of the Church and the world is yours to develop. God has put his trust in you, because he knows and loves you. How will you answer his trust and love?

Michael Hollings
(1921–1997)

Daily Prayer

An ordinary person is a person of habit. So many things we do, like breathing, eating and sleeping, we do almost without thinking. But they are essential to our living. Prayer can, and should, become a habit during a busy or empty day, a sleepless night – but it must be practised. One very good habit is to begin and end each day with prayer.

Practice is necessary so that prayer becomes as much a habit as breathing. This may well mean you decide on a prayer, or a series of times to pause during the day to think of God. Do this practice regularly, until it is so much a part of you that your chosen prayer comes to the surface any time you are at peace or doing nothing, in danger, distress and so on.

The following short prayers are well-tried and well-loved examples. One word is quite enough. Find and possess your own.

Jesus – God – Love
God loves me

My Lord and my God
Lord, he whom you love is sick
Lord Jesus Christ, Son of God, have mercy
on me a sinner
Jesus, mercy; Mary, help
Into your hands, O Lord, I commend my spirit
O God, take heed and save me; O Lord,
make haste and help me.

There are certain prayers which are known and loved by all Catholics. Here are some.

In the name of the Father, and of the Son, and of the Holy Spirit. Amen.

Our Father

Our Father, who art in heaven,
hallowed be thy name.
Thy kingdom come. Thy will be done on earth,
as it is in heaven.
Give us this day our daily bread,
and forgive us our trespasses,
as we forgive those who trespass against us. And lead
us not into temptation,
but deliver us from evil.
Amen.

Many Christians use another version of the prayer Our Lord taught us. Here it is:

Our Father in heaven,
hallowed be your name,
your kingdom come,
your will be done,

on earth as in heaven.
Give us today our daily bread.
Forgive us our sins
as we forgive those who sin against us.
Save us from the time of trial
and deliver us from evil.
Amen.

Hail, Mary

Hail Mary, full of grace,
the Lord is with thee:
blessed art thou amongst women,
and blessed is the fruit of thy womb, Jesus.
Holy Mary, Mother of God,
pray for us sinners,
now and at the hour of our death. Amen.

Glory Be

Glory be to the Father,
and to the Son,
and to the Holy Spirit,
as it was in the beginning,
is now, and ever shall be,
world without end. Amen.

The Apostles' Creed

I believe in God,
the Father almighty,
creator of heaven and earth.
I believe in Jesus Christ,
his only Son, our Lord.
He was conceived by the power of the Holy Spirit,
and born of the Virgin Mary.
He suffered under Pontius Pilate,
was crucified, died and was buried.
He descended to the dead.
On the third day he rose again.
He ascended into heaven,
and is seated at the right hand of the Father.
I believe in the Holy Spirit,
the holy Catholic Church,
the communion of Saints,
the resurrection of the body,
and the life everlasting.
Amen.

Much of our prayer must be concerned with daily life and the situations we find there, with our moods and feelings about people, our situation in the world. The prayers which follow have been used by Catholics and other Christians over the years to help them in their everyday contact with God and their fellow human beings.

Morning Offering

O Jesus, through the most pure heart of Mary, I offer you all the prayers, thoughts, works and sufferings of this day.

Act of Contrition

O my God, because you are so good, I am very sorry that I have sinned against you, and by the help of your grace I will try not to sin again.

or

God our Father,
I thank you for loving me.
I am sorry for all my sins,
for what I have done and
for what I have failed to do.
I will sincerely try to love you and others
in everything I do and say.
Help me to walk in your light today
and always.

Act of Faith

My God, I believe in you and all that your Church teaches, because you have said it, and your word is true.

Act of Hope

My God, I hope in you, for grace and for glory, because of your promises, your mercy and power.

Act of Charity

O my God, I love you with my whole heart and above all things, because you are infinitely good and perfect; and I love my neighbour as myself for love of you. Grant that I may love you more and more in this life, and in the next for all eternity.

Prayer to our Guardian Angel

O angel of God, appointed by divine mercy to be my guardian, enlighten and protect, direct and govern me this day.

Grace at meals

Bless us, O Lord, and these your gifts which we are about to receive by your goodness, through Christ our Lord. Amen.

or

Bless, Lord, this food you give us.
As we eat it, help us to think of those who are hungry,
to be sparing in satisfying our appetites,
and thoughtful for those who are still hungry,
not just in ideas,
but in action for freedom,
peace and justice. Amen.

or

We give you thanks, almighty God, for these and all your gifts which we have received through Christ our Lord. Amen.

The Grace

The grace of our Lord Jesus Christ and the love of God, and the fellowship of the Holy Spirit, be with us all evermore. Amen.

An Evening Prayer

O my God, I thank you for all the benefits which I have ever received from you, and especially this day. Give me light to see what sins I have committed, and grant me grace to be truly sorry for them.

Nunc Dimittis

At last, all powerful Master,
you give leave to your servant to go in peace,
according to your promise.
For my eyes have seen your salvation
which you have prepared for all nations,
the light to enlighten the Gentiles
and give glory to Israel, your people.
Give praise to the Father almighty,

to his Son, Jesus Christ, the Lord,
to the Spirit, who dwells in our hearts,
both now and forever. Amen.

Prayer to the Holy Spirit

Come, Holy Spirit, fill the hearts of your faithful, and
enkindle in them the fire of your love.
Send forth your Spirit and they shall be created.
And you shall renew the face of the earth.
Let us pray: O God, who has taught the hearts of the
faithful by the light of the Holy Spirit, grant that by
the gift of the same Spirit we may be always truly wise
and ever rejoice in his consolation.

Spirit of the Living God

Spirit of the living God,
fall afresh on me.
Break me, melt me,
mould me, fill me.
Spirit of the living God,
fall afresh on me.

© Daniel Iverson, Birdwing Music, Alliance Media Ltd.
Administered by Copycare.

Prayer for Dedication

Lord Jesus

I give you my hands to do your work.
I give you my feet to go your way.
I give you my eyes to see as you do.
I give you my tongue to speak your words.
I give you my mind that you may think in me.
I give you my spirit that you may pray in me.

Above all
 I give you my heart that you may love in me,
 your Father, and all mankind.
 I give you my whole self that you may grow in me,
 so that it is you, Lord Jesus,
 who lives and works and prays in me.

Prayer of Dedication

O God, to whom all hearts are open, all desires known,
and from whom no secrets are hidden, cleanse the
thoughts of our hearts by the inpouring of your Holy
Spirit, that every thought and word of ours may begin
from you, and in you be perfectly completed, through
Christ our Lord.

Prayer for Peace

O God, source of holy desires, right counsels and just
actions, grant to your servants that peace which the
world cannot give, so that our hearts may be wholly
devoted to your service, and all our days, freed from
dread of our enemies, may be passed in quietness under your protection.

Prayer for Unity

Lord Jesus Christ, you said to your apostles,
'I leave you peace, my peace I give you'.
Look not on our sins but on the faith of your Church
and grant us the peace and unity of your kingdom
where you live for ever and ever.

Muslim Prayer

O God! O God! We ask that you will turn away our faces from any other goal than yourself, and grant us to gaze towards your noble countenance until we see you in everything.

A Prayer when distracted

When the heart is hard and parched up, come upon me with a shower of mercy.

When grace is lost from life, come with a burst of song.

When tumultuous work raises its din on all sides shutting me out from beyond, come to me, my Lord of silence, with thy peace and rest.

When my beggarly heart sits crouched, shut up in a corner, break open the door, my king, and come with the ceremony of a king.

When desire blinds the mind with delusion and dust, O thou holy one, thou wakeful, come with thy light and thy thunder.

Rabindranath Tagore (1861-1941)

17

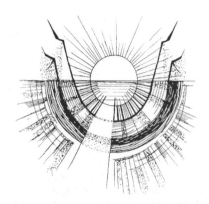

God be in my head

> God be in my head, and in my understanding;
> God be in mine eyes, and in my looking;
> God be in my mouth, and in my speaking;
> God be in my heart, and in my thinking;
> God be at mine end, and at my departing.

Book of Hours (1514)

Prayer of Cardinal Newman

> May he support us all the day long, till the shades lengthen and the evening comes, and the busy world is hushed and the fever of life is over and our work is done. Then in his mercy may he give us a safe lodging and a holy rest and peace at the last.

Prayer of St Francis of Assisi

>Lord, make me an instrument of your peace:
>>where there is hatred let me sow peace,
>>where there is injury let me sow pardon,
>>where there is doubt let me sow faith,
>>where there is despair let me give hope,
>>where there is darkness let me give light,
>
>O Divine Master, grant that I may
>>not try to be comforted but to comfort,
>>not try to be understood but to understand,
>>not try to be loved but to love.
>
>Because it is in giving that we receive,
>it is in forgiving that we are forgiven,
>and it is in dying that we are born to eternal life.

Prayer of St Richard of Chichester

>Thanks be to you, my Lord Jesus Christ, for all the benefits and blessings which you have given to me, for all the pains and insults which you have borne for me, O most merciful Friend, Brother and Redeemer. May I know you more clearly, love you more dearly, and follow you more nearly.

>*or a modern version of this prayer*
>
>Day by day,
>O dear Lord,
>three things I pray:
>to see you more clearly,
>love you more dearly,
>follow you more nearly,
>day by day,
>by day by day.

Prayer of St Ignatius

Take, Lord, of all my liberty. Receive my memory, my understanding, and my whole will. Whatever I have and possess, you have given me; to you, I restore it wholly, and to your will I utterly surrender it for my direction. Give me the love of you only, with your grace, and I am rich enough; nor do I ask anything beside.

or another version of this prayer

Teach us, good Lord, to serve you as you deserve;
to give and not to count the cost;
to fight and not heed the wounds;
to toil, and not to seek for rest;
to labour and to ask for no reward, save that
    of knowing that we do your will;
through Jesus Christ our Lord.

St Francis of Assisi's prayer before the crucifix

Most high, glorious God,
enlighten the darkness of my heart
and give me, Lord,
a correct faith,
certain hope, perfect charity,
sense and knowledge
so that I may perfectly carry out
Your holy and true command.

Anima Christi

Soul of Christ, sanctify me.
Body of Christ, heal me.
Blood of Christ, drench me.
Water from the side of Christ, wash me.

Passion of Christ, strengthen me.
Good Jesus, hear me.

In your wounds shelter me.
From turning away keep me.
From the evil one protect me.
At the hour of my death call me.
Into your presence lead me,
to praise you with all your saints
for ever and ever. Amen.

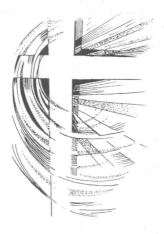

The Angelus

The Angel of the Lord declared to Mary:
and she conceived of the Holy Spirit.
Hail Mary, …

Behold the handmaid of the Lord:
be it done to me according to your word.
Hail Mary, …

And the Word was made flesh:
and dwelt among us.
Hail Mary, …

Pray for us, O holy Mother of God.
That we may be made worthy of the promises of
Christ.

Let us pray: pour forth, we beseech you, O Lord, your
grace into our hearts that we, to whom the incarnation
of Christ, your Son, was made known by the message
of an angel, may be brought by his passion and cross †
to the glory of his resurrection, through the same Christ
our Lord. Amen.

May the divine assistance remain always with us † and
may the souls of the faithful departed, through the
mercy of God, rest in peace. Amen.

The Memorare

Remember, O most loving Virgin Mary, that it is a thing
unheard of, that anyone ever had recourse to your protection, implored your help, or sought your intercession, and was left forsaken. Filled therefore with confidence in your goodness I fly to you, O Mother, Vir-

gin of virgins. To you I come, before you I stand, a sorrowful sinner. Despise not my poor words, O Mother of the Word of God, but graciously hear and grant my prayer.

Hail, Holy Queen

Hail, holy queen, mother of mercy; hail, our life, our sweetness, and our hope! To you do we cry, poor banished children of Eve. To you do we send up our sighs, mourning and weeping in this vale of tears. Turn then, most gracious advocate, your eyes of mercy towards us; and after this our exile, show to us the blessed fruit of your womb, Jesus.

O clement, O loving, O sweet Virgin Mary.

Pray for us, O holy Mother of God.

That we may be made worthy of the promises of Christ.

This prayer follows the *Hail, Holy Queen* when the Rosary has been said.

Let us pray: O God, whose only-begotten Son, by his life, death and resurrection, has purchased for us the rewards of eternal life; grant, we beseech you, that, meditating upon these mysteries, in the most holy Rosary of the Blessed Virgin Mary, we may both imitate what they contain, and obtain what they promise. Through the same Christ our Lord. Amen.

Act of resignation

O Lord, my God, from this moment do I accept from your hands, with a quiet and trusting heart, whatsoever death you shall choose to send me with its pains and griefs.

For the faithful departed (*The De Profundis*)

Out of the depths I cry to you, O Lord,
Lord, hear my voice!
O Let your ears be attentive
to the voice of my pleading.

If you, O Lord, should mark our guilt,
Lord, who would survive?
But with you is found forgiveness:
for this we revere you.

My soul is waiting for the Lord,
I count on his word.
My soul is longing for the Lord
more than watchmen for daybreak.

Because with the Lord there is mercy
and fullness of redemption.
Israel indeed he will redeem
from all its iniquity.

Eternal rest grant unto them, O Lord.
And let perpetual light shine upon them.
May they rest in peace.

May the souls of all the faithful departed,
through the mercy of God,
rest in peace. Amen.

The Order of Mass

Jesus said "When two or three are gathered in my name I shall be with them." This is especially so when we gather for mass. Jesus comes to us in so many ways. He comes to us in the whole community gathered for prayer. He comes to us in the sacred scriptures. He comes to us in the ministry of the priest. He comes to us above all in the bread and wine that become his body and blood, holy food for a holy people.

INTRODUCTORY RITES

When the people have assembled the priest and ministers go to the altar. A hymn may be sung, otherwise the Entrance Antiphon is recited.

Everyone makes the sign of the cross as the priest says:

In the name of the Father, and of the Son,
and of the Holy Spirit.
Amen.

The priest says the following or another greeting taken from the Roman Missal:

> The grace of our Lord Jesus Christ and the love of God
>   and the fellowship of the Holy Spirit be with you all.

All respond:
And also with you.

The priest invites the people to repentance in these or similar words:

> My brothers and sisters,
> to prepare ourselves to celebrate the sacred mysteries,
> let us call to mind our sins.

After a brief silence there follows one of the forms of the Penitential Rite.

**1   I confess to almighty God,
    and to you, my brothers and sisters,
    that I have sinned through my own fault**
            all strike their breast
    **in my thoughts and in my words,
    in what I have done,
    and in what I have failed to do;
    and I ask blessed Mary, ever virgin,
    all the angels and saints,
    and you, my brothers and sisters,
    to pray for me to the Lord our God.**

The priest says the absolution.

> May almighty God have mercy on us,
> forgive us our sins
> and bring us to everlasting life. **Amen.**

Lord, have mercy.	**Lord, have mercy.**
Christ, have mercy.	**Christ, have mercy.**
Lord, have mercy.	**Lord, have mercy.**

Turn to page 28 for the Gloria

2   Lord, we have sinned against you:
Lord, have mercy.
Lord, have mercy.

Lord, show us your mercy and love.
And grant us your salvation.

May almighty God have mercy on us,
forgive us our sins,
and bring us to everlasting life. **Amen**.

Lord, have mercy.	**Lord, have mercy.**
Christ, have mercy.	**Christ, have mercy.**
Lord, have mercy.	**Lord, have mercy.**

Turn to page 28 for the Gloria

3   You were sent to heal the contrite:*
Lord, have mercy.
Lord, have mercy.

You came to call sinners:
Christ, have mercy.
Christ have mercy.

You plead for us at the right hand of the Father:
Lord, have mercy.
Lord, have mercy.

* Other invocations may be used.

May almighty God have mercy on us,
forgive us our sins, and bring us to everlasting life.
Amen.

THE GLORIA

This hymn of praise is omitted in Advent and Lent.

Glory to God in the highest,
and peace to his people on earth.

Lord God, heavenly King,
almighty God and Father,
we worship you, we give you thanks,
we praise you for your glory.
Lord Jesus Christ, only Son of the Father
Lord God, Lamb of God,
you take away the sin of the world:
have mercy on us;
you are seated at the right hand of the Father:
receive our prayer.

For you alone are the Holy One,
you alone are the Lord,
you alone are the Most High,
Jesus Christ,
with the Holy Spirit
in the glory of God the Father. Amen.

OPENING PRAYER

The priest invites everyone to pray, and will often give an indication of a particular theme for the prayer, for example 'That God will make us more like Christ his Son'. All pray in silence, and then the priest will gather all our prayers together in the Opening or Collect Prayer.

LITURGY OF THE WORD

In the Liturgy of the Word, God speaks anew to his people and they respond in prayer. In one way or another the lesson of the readings is meant to sink into us. This can be helped by a homily (a few words on the meaning and message). A little used but excellent way is a period of silence for reflection. After the readings and homily all stand for the Creed.

CREED
> **We believe in one God,**
> > **the Father, the Almighty,**
> > **maker of heaven and earth,**
> > **of all that is, seen and unseen.**
>
> **We believe in one Lord Jesus Christ,**
> > **the only Son of God,**
> > **eternally begotten of the Father,**
> > **God from God, Light from Light,**
> > **true God from true God,**
> > **begotten, not made,**
> > **of one Being with the Father.**
> > **Through him all things were made.**
> > **For us men and for our salvation**
> > **he came down from heaven: all bow**
> > > (at Christmas and the Annunciation, kneel)
> > **by the power of the Holy Spirit**
> > > **he became incarnate from the Virgin Mary,**
> > > **and was made man.**
> > **For our sake he was crucified under Pontius Pilate;**
> > > **he suffered death and was buried.**
> > > **On the third day he rose again**
> > > > **in accordance with the Scriptures;**

he ascended into heaven
  and is seated at the right hand of the Father.
He will come again in glory to judge the living
  and the dead, and his kingdom will have no end.

We believe in the Holy Spirit, the Lord, the giver
    of life,
  who proceeds from the Father and the Son.
  With the Father and the Son he is worshipped
    and glorified.
  He has spoken through the Prophets.
  We believe in one holy catholic and apostolic
    Church.
  We acknowledge one baptism for the
    forgiveness of sins.
  We look for the resurrection of the dead.
    and the life of the world to come. Amen.

PRAYERS OF THE FAITHFUL

The whole assembly now prays for the needs of the world, the Church and the local community. A series of intentions is presented to guide the prayer, after each of which all say:

Hear our prayer

or   **Lord, graciously hear us**

or any other customary phrase.
A prayer by the priest concludes and all answer: **Amen.**

THE LITURGY OF THE EUCHARIST

Having listened to the 'great works of God' in the Scriptures, we give thanks in the way Christ taught us, following his command to 'take, bless, break and eat' in memory of Him.

PREPARATION OF THE ALTAR AND GIFTS

The offerings are brought to the altar. The assembly may sing a hymn, which may continue while the priest says the following prayers in silence. If there is no hymn the priest may say the prayers aloud and all make the response.

> Blessed are you, Lord, God of all creation.
> Through your goodness we have this bread to offer,
> which earth has given and human hands have made.
> It will become for us the bread of life.
> **Blessed be God for ever.**

As the priest adds a little water to the chalice, he says quietly:

> By the mystery of this water and wine may we come to share in the divinity of Christ, who humbled himself to share in our humanity.

He continues aloud:

> Blessed are you, Lord, God of all creation.
> Through your goodness we have this wine to offer,
> fruit of the vine and work of human hands.
> It will become our spiritual drink.
> **Blessed be God for ever.**

As the priest makes his private prayers of preparation, we too recollect what we are about to do, and ask the Lord to make us ready to praise him for the great gift of Jesus' life, death and resurrection.

The priest says quietly:

> Lord God, we ask you to receive us and be pleased with the sacrifice we offer you with humble and contrite hearts.

The priest washes his hands, saying quietly:

> Lord, wash away my iniquity;
> cleanse me from my sin.

He invites the people to prayer:

> Pray, brethren, that our sacrifice
>   (*or* Pray, brethren, that my sacrifice and yours)
> may be acceptable to God the almighty Father.

> **May the Lord accept the sacrifice at your hands,**
> **for the praise and glory of his name,**
> **for our good, and the good of all his Church.**

PRAYER OVER THE GIFTS

The priest prays the final preparatory prayer, the brief Prayer over the Gifts.

THE EUCHARISTIC PRAYER

In the Eucharistic Prayer the whole assembly unites to praise and give thanks to God and to offer sacrifice.

There are four principal Eucharistic prayers in the Roman Catholic Rite. There are in addition other Eucharistic prayers approved for use when appropriate, for example the Eucharistic prayers for masses with children, masses with the deaf, for reconciliation and for masses for various needs and occasions. Only the four principal ones are given here.

The first section of most of the Eucharistic prayers, called the Preface, varies according to the day or season. Some Eucharistic prayers, such as Eucharistic Prayer 4, have fixed prefaces which must always be used.

The whole prayer is of great solemnity. As we pray it we remember Jesus at the Last Supper asking us to 'do this in memory of me'; we remember his self-offering at Calvary; and we remember his resurrection and ascension. We praise God the Father for these wonders. In the praying of the prayer Jesus is again present for us in the bread and wine that becomes his body and blood, offered in thanksgiving to the Father and shared amongst us in Holy Communion.

Opening Dialogue

The Lord be with you. **And also with you.**
Lift up your hearts. **We lift them up to the Lord.**
Let us give thanks to
    the Lord our God. **It is right to give him
        thanks and praise.**

The priest then begins the Preface to the Eucharistic Prayer,
a prayer of thanks and praise. At the end everyone says or
sings:

**Holy, holy, holy Lord, God of power and might,
heaven and earth are full of your glory.
    Hosanna in the highest.
Blessed is he who comes in the name of the Lord.
    Hosanna in the highest.**

Turn to:
page 35 for Eucharistic Prayer 1
page 40 for Eucharistic Prayer 2
page 43 for Eucharistic Prayer 3
page 47 for Eucharistic Prayer 4

EUCHARISTIC PRAYER 1

(THE ROMAN CANON)

We come to you, Father,
with praise and thanksgiving,
through Jesus Christ your Son.
Through him we ask you to accept and bless
these gifts we offer you in sacrifice.
We offer them for your holy catholic Church,
watch over it, Lord, and guide it;
grant it peace and unity throughout the world.
We offer them for *N.* our Pope,
for *N.* our bishop,
and for all who hold and teach the catholic faith
that comes to us from the apostles.
Remember, Lord, your people,
especially those for whom we now pray, *N.* and *N.*
Remember all of us gathered here before you.
You know how firmly we believe in you
and dedicate ourselves to you.
We offer you this sacrifice of praise
for ourselves and those who are dear to us.
We pray to you, our living and true God,
for our well-being and redemption.

In union with the whole Church * [*see page 36*]
we honour Mary,
the ever-virgin mother of Jesus Christ our Lord and God.
We honour Joseph, her husband,
the apostles and martyrs
Peter and Paul, Andrew,

(James, John, Thomas,
James, Philip,
Bartholomew, Matthew, Simon and Jude;
we honour Linus, Cletus, Clement, Sixtus,
Cornelius, Cyprian, Lawrence, Chrysogonus,
John and Paul, Cosmas and Damian)
and all the saints.
May their merits and prayers
gain us your constant help and protection.
(Through Christ our Lord. Amen.)

* Pentecost

In union with the whole Church
we celebrate the day of Pentecost
when the Holy Spirit appeared to the apostles
in the form of countless tongues.
We honour Mary…

Father, accept this offering from your whole family.
Grant us your peace in this life,
save us from final damnation,
and count us among those you have chosen.

Bless and approve our offering,
make it acceptable to you,
an offering in spirit and in truth.
let it become for us
the body and blood of Jesus Christ,
your only Son, our Lord.

The day before he suffered
he took bread in his sacred hands
and looking up to heaven,

to you, his almighty Father,
he gave you thanks and praise.
He broke the bread,
gave it to his disciples, and said:

> TAKE THIS, ALL OF YOU, AND EAT EAT:
> THIS IS MY BODY WHICH WILL BE GIVEN UP
> FOR YOU.

When supper was ended
he took the cup.
Again he gave you thanks and praise,
gave the cup to his disciples, and said:

> TAKE THIS, ALL OF YOU, AND DRINK FROM IT:
> THIS IS THE CUP OF MY BLOOD,
> THE BLOOD OF THE NEW
> AND EVERLASTING COVENANT.
> IT WILL BE SHED FOR YOU AND FOR ALL
> SO THAT SINS MAY BE FORGIVEN.
> DO THIS IN MEMORY OF ME.

The priest (or the deacon, if there is one) says or sings:
Let us proclaim the mystery of faith:
1   **Christ has died,**
    Christ is risen,
    Christ will come again.

Alternative acclamations
2   **Dying you destroyed our death,**
    rising you restored our life.
    Lord Jesus, come in glory.

3   **When we eat this bread and drink this cup,**
    we proclaim your death, Lord Jesus,
    until you come in glory.

**4   Lord, by your cross and resurrection
you have set us free.
You are the Saviour of the world.**

Father, we celebrate the memory of Christ, your Son.
We, your people and your ministers,
recall his passion,
his resurrection from the dead,
and his ascension into glory;
and from the many gifts you have given us
we offer to you, God of glory and majesty,
this holy and perfect sacrifice:
the bread of life
and the cup of eternal salvation.

Look with favour on these offerings
and accept them as once you accepted the gifts of your
        servant Abel,
the sacrifice of Abraham, our father in faith,
and the bread and wine offered by your priest
        Melchisedech.
Almighty God,
we pray that your angel may take this sacrifice
to your altar in heaven.
Then, as we receive from this altar
the sacred body and blood of your Son,
let us be filled with every grace and blessing.
        (Through Christ our Lord. Amen.)

Remember, Lord, those who have died
and have gone before us marked with
        the sign of faith,
especially those for whom we now pray, *N.* and *N.*
May these, and all who sleep in Christ,

find in your presence
light, happiness, and peace.
    (Through Christ our Lord. Amen.)

For ourselves, too, we ask
some share in the fellowship of your apostles and
martyrs, with John the Baptist, Stephen, Matthias,
Barnabas, (Ignatius, Alexander, Marcellinus, Peter,
Felicity, Perpetua, Agatha, Lucy, Agnes, Cecilia,
Anastasia)
and all the saints.

Though we are sinners,
we trust in your mercy and love.
Do not consider what we truly deserve,
but grant us your forgiveness.

Through Christ our Lord
you give us all these gifts.
You fill them with life and goodness,
you bless them and make them holy.

Through him,
with him,
in him,
in the unity of the Holy Spirit,
all glory and honour is yours,
almighty Father,
for ever and ever.
Amen.

Continue on page 51

EUCHARISTIC PRAYER 2

The Lord be with you. **And also with you.**
Lift up your hearts. **We lift them up to the Lord.**
Let us give thanks to
    the Lord our God. **It is right to give him
              thanks and praise.**

Father, it is our duty and our salvation,
always and everywhere
to give you thanks
through your beloved Son, Jesus Christ.
He is the Word through whom you made the universe,
the Saviour you sent to redeem us.
By the power of the Holy Spirit
he took flesh and was born of the Virgin Mary.
For our sake he opened his arms on the cross;
he put an end to death
and revealed the resurrection.
In this he fulfilled your will
and won for you a holy people.
And so we join with the angels and the saints
in proclaiming your glory
as we sing/say:

**Holy, holy, holy Lord, God of power and might,
heaven and earth are full of your glory.
    Hosanna in the highest.
Blessed is he who comes in the name of the Lord.
    Hosanna in the highest.**

Lord, you are holy indeed,
the fountain of all holiness.

Let your Spirit come upon these gifts to make them holy,
so that they may become for us
the body and blood of our Lord, Jesus Christ.

Before he was given up to death,
a death he freely accepted,
he took bread and gave you thanks.
He broke the bread,
gave it to his disciples, and said:

> TAKE THIS, ALL OF YOU, AND EAT IT:
> THIS IS MY BODY WHICH WILL BE GIVEN UP
> FOR YOU.

When supper was ended, he took the cup.
Again he gave you thanks and praise,
gave the cup to his disciples, and said:

> TAKE THIS, ALL OF YOU, AND DRINK FROM IT:
> THIS IS THE CUP OF MY BLOOD,
> THE BLOOD OF THE NEW AND
> EVERLASTING COVENANT.
> IT WILL BE SHED FOR YOU AND FOR ALL
> SO THAT SINS MAY BE FORGIVEN.
> DO THIS IN MEMORY OF ME.

The priest (or the deacon, if there is one) says or sings:

Let us proclaim the mystery of faith:
1   **Christ has died,**
    Christ is risen,
    Christ will come again.

Alternative acclamations

2   **Dying you destroyed our death,**
    rising you restored our life.
    Lord Jesus, come in glory.

**3   When we eat this bread and drink this cup,
      we proclaim your death, Lord Jesus,
      until you come in glory.**

**4   Lord, by your cross and resurrection
      you have set us free.
      You are the Saviour of the world.**

In memory of his death and resurrection,
we offer you, Father, this life-giving bread, this
      saving cup.
We thank you for counting us worthy
to stand in your presence and serve you.
May all of us who share in the body and blood of Christ
be brought together in unity by the Holy Spirit.

Lord, remember your Church throughout the world;
make us grow in love,
together with *N*. our Pope, *N*. our bishop,
and all the clergy.

In Masses for the Dead, the following may be added:

Remember *N*., whom you have called from this life.
In baptism he (she) died with Christ:
may he (she) also share his resurrection.

Remember our brothers and sisters
who have gone to their rest
in the hope of rising again;
bring them and all the departed
into the light of your presence.

Have mercy on us all;
make us worthy to share eternal life
with Mary, the virgin Mother of God,

with the apostles, and with all the saints
who have done your will throughout the ages.
May we praise you in union with them,
and give you glory
through your Son, Jesus Christ.

Through him,
with him,
in him,
in the unity of the Holy Spirit,
all glory and honour is yours,
almighty Father,
for ever and ever.
Amen.   *Continue on page 51*

EUCHARISTIC PRAYER 3

Father, you are holy indeed,
and all creation rightly gives you praise.
All life, all holiness comes from you
through your Son, Jesus Christ our Lord,
by the working of the Holy Spirit.
From age to age you gather a people to yourself,
so that from east to west
a perfect offering may be made
to the glory of your name.

And so, Father, we bring you these gifts.
We ask you to make them holy by the power of your
Spirit,
that they may become the body and blood
of your Son, our Lord Jesus Christ,
at whose command we celebrate this eucharist.

On the night he was betrayed,
he took bread and gave you thanks and praise.
He broke the bread, gave it to his disciples, and said:

> TAKE THIS, ALL OF YOU, AND EAT IT:
>> THIS IS MY BODY WHICH WILL BE GIVEN
>> UP FOR YOU.

When supper was ended, he took the cup.
Again he gave you thanks and praise,
gave the cup to his disciples, and said:

> TAKE THIS, ALL OF YOU, AND DRINK FROM IT:
> THIS IS THE CUP OF MY BLOOD,
> THE BLOOD OF THE NEW AND
> EVERLASTING COVENANT.
> IT WILL BE SHED FOR YOU AND FOR ALL
> SO THAT SINS MAY BE FORGIVEN.
> DO THIS IN MEMORY OF ME.

The priest (or the deacon, if there is one) says or sings:

Let us proclaim the mystery of faith:

**1 Christ has died,
Christ is risen,
Christ will come again.**

Alternative acclamations

**2 Dying you destroyed our death,
rising you restored our life.
Lord Jesus, come in glory.**

**3 When we eat this bread and drink this cup,
we proclaim your death, Lord Jesus,
until you come in glory.**

**4   Lord, by your cross and resurrection
you have set us free.
You are the Saviour of the world.**

Father, calling to mind the death your Son endured
    for our salvation,
his glorious resurrection and ascension into heaven,
and ready to greet him when he comes again,
we offer you in thanksgiving this holy and living sacrifice.

Look with favour on your Church's offering,
and see the Victim whose death has reconciled us
    to yourself.
Grant that we, who are nourished by his body and blood,
may be filled with his Holy Spirit,
and become one body, one spirit in Christ.
May he make us an everlasting gift to you
and enable us to share in the inheritance of your saints,
with Mary, the virgin Mother of God;
with the apostles, the martyrs,
(Saint *N. – the patron saint or saint of the day)*
    and all your saints.
on whose constant intercession we rely for help.

Lord, may this sacrifice,
which has made our peace with you,
advance the peace and salvation of all the world.
Strengthen in faith and love your pilgrim Church on earth;
your servant, Pope *N.*, our bishop *N.*,
and all the bishops,
with the clergy and the entire people your Son
    has gained for you.

Father, hear the prayers of the family you have
    gathered here before you.
In mercy and love unite all your children
wherever they may be.*
Welcome into your kingdom our departed brothers
    and sisters,
and all who have left this world in your friendship.
We hope to enjoy for ever the vision of your glory,
through Christ our Lord, from whom all good things come.

Through him,
with him,
in him,
in the unity of the Holy Spirit
all glory and honour is yours,
almighty Father,
for ever and ever. **Amen.**

Continue on page 51

---

* In Masses for the Dead the following ending may be used.

Remember *N*.
In baptism he (she) died with Christ:
may he (she) share his resurrection
when Christ will raise our mortal bodies
and make them like his own in glory.
Welcome into your kingdom our departed
    brothers and sisters,
and all who have left this world in your friendship.
There we hope to share in your glory
when every tear will be wiped away.
On that day we shall see you, our God, as you are.
We shall become like you
and praise you for ever through Christ our Lord,
from whom all good things come.

EUCHARISTIC PRAYER 4

When this Eucharistic Prayer is used the following Preface is
always said.

Father in heaven,
it is right that we should give you thanks and glory:
you alone are God, living and true.
Through all eternity you live in unapproachable light.
Source of life and goodness, you have created all things,
to fill your creatures with every blessing
and lead all men to the joyful vision of your light.

Countless hosts of angels stand before you to do your will;
they look upon your splendour
and praise you, night and day.

United with them,
and in the name of every creature under heaven,
we too praise your glory as we sing/say:

Holy, holy, holy Lord, God of power and might,
heaven and earth are full of your glory.
   Hosanna in the highest.
Blessed is he who comes in the name of the Lord.
   Hosanna in the highest.

Father, we acknowledge your greatness:
all your actions show your wisdom and love.
You formed man in your own likeness
and set him over the whole world
to serve you, his creator,
and to rule over all creatures.
Even when he disobeyed you and lost your friendship
you did not abandon him to the power of death,

but helped all men to seek and find you.
Again and again you offered a covenant to man,
and through the prophets taught him to hope for salvation.
Father, you so loved the world
that in the fullness of time you sent your only Son to be
    our Saviour.
He was conceived through the power of the Holy Spirit,
and born of the Virgin Mary,
a man like us in all things but sin.
To the poor he proclaimed the good news of salvation,
to prisoners, freedom,
and to those in sorrow, joy.
In fulfilment of your will
he gave himself up to death;
but by rising from the dead,
he destroyed death and restored life.
And that we might live no longer for ourselves but for
him,
he sent the Holy Spirit from you, Father,
as his first gift to those who believe,
to complete his work on earth
and bring us the fullness of grace.

Father, may this Holy Spirit sanctify these offerings.
Let them become the body and blood of Jesus Christ
    our Lord
as we celebrate the great mystery
which he left us as an everlasting covenant.

He always loved those who were his own in the world.
When the time came for him to be glorified by you,
    his heavenly Father,
he showed the depth of his love.

While they were at supper,
he took bread, said the blessing, broke the bread,
and gave it to his disciples, saying:

> TAKE THIS, ALL OF YOU, AND EAT IT:
> THIS IS MY BODY WHICH WILL BE GIVEN
> UP FOR YOU.

In the same way, he took the cup, filled with wine.
He gave you thanks, and giving the cup to his
disciples, said:

> TAKE THIS, ALL OF YOU, AND DRINK FROM IT:
> THIS IS THE CUP OF MY BLOOD,
> THE BLOOD OF THE NEW AND
> EVERLASTING COVENANT.
> IT WILL BE SHED FOR YOU AND FOR ALL
> SO THAT SINS MAY BE FORGIVEN.
> DO THIS IN MEMORY OF ME.

The priest (or the deacon, if there is one) says or sings:

Let us proclaim the mystery of faith:

**1 Christ has died,
Christ is risen,
Christ will come again.**

Alternative acclamations

**2 Dying you destroyed our death,
rising you restored our life.
Lord Jesus, come in glory.**

**3 When we eat this bread and drink this cup,
we proclaim your death, Lord Jesus,
until you come in glory.**

4 **Lord, by your cross and resurrection**
you have set us free.
You are the Saviour of the world.

Father, we now celebrate this memorial
　　of our redemption.
We recall Christ's death, his descent among the dead,
his resurrection, and his ascension to your right hand;
and, looking forward to his coming in glory,
we offer you his body and blood,
the acceptable sacrifice
which brings salvation to the whole world.

Lord, look upon this sacrifice which you have
　　given to your Church;
and by your Holy Spirit, gather all who share
　　this one bread and one cup
into the one body of Christ, a living sacrifice of praise.

Lord, remember those for whom we offer this sacrifice,
especially *N.* our Pope,
N. our bishop, and bishops and clergy everywhere.
Remember those who take part in this offering,
those here present and all your people,
and all who seek you with a sincere heart.
Remember those who have died in the peace of Christ
and all the dead whose faith is known to you alone.
Father, in your mercy grant also to us, your children,
to enter into our heavenly inheritance
in the company of the Virgin Mary, the Mother of God,
and your apostles and saints.
Then, in your kingdom,
freed from the corruption of sin and death,

we shall sing your glory with every creature through
  Christ our Lord,
through whom you give us everything that is good.

Through him,
with him,
in him,
in the unity of the Holy Spirit,
all glory and honour is yours,
almighty Father,
for ever and ever.
Amen.

The Communion Rite

THE LORD'S PRAYER

The priest invites everyone to join in the Lord's Prayer in
these or similar words:

Let us pray with confidence to the Father in the words
our Saviour gave us:

Our Father, who art in heaven,
hallowed be thy name.
Thy kingdom come,
thy will be done
on earth as it is in heaven.
Give us this day our daily bread,
and forgive us our trespasses
as we forgive those who trespass against us,
and lead us not into temptation
but deliver us from evil.

Deliver us, Lord, from every evil,
and grant us peace in our day.
In your mercy keep us free from sin
and protect us from all anxiety
as we wait in joyful hope
for the coming of our Saviour, Jesus Christ.

**For the kingdom, the power and the glory are yours,
now and for ever.**

PRAYER AND SIGN OF PEACE

Lord Jesus Christ, you said to your apostles:
I leave you peace, my peace I give you.
Look not on our sins, but on the faith of your Church,
and grant us the peace and unity of your kingdom
where you live for ever and ever.
Amen.

The peace of the Lord be with you always.
And also with you.

Then the deacon, or the priest, may add:

Let us offer each other the sign of peace.

Now we acknowledge publicly that we want to be at peace
together in unity and fellowship. The Church suggests we show
this desire by greeting each other. We can do this in several
ways – with a smile, a handshake, or any friendly gesture.

THE BREAKING OF BREAD

The priest breaks the bread that has become the Body of the Lord so that it can be distributed in communion. He places a small piece in the chalice saying:

> May this mingling of the body and blood of our Lord Jesus Christ bring eternal life to us who receive it.

Meanwhile the following is sung or said:

> **Lamb of God, you take away the sins of the world: have mercy on us.**
> **Lamb of God, you take away the sins of the world: have mercy on us.**
> **Lamb of God, you take away the sins of the world: grant us peace.**

PREPARATION FOR COMMUNION

The priest says quietly while we too make these or similar prayers:

> Lord Jesus Christ, Son of the living God, by the will of the Father and the work of the Holy Spirit your death brought life to the world. By your holy body and blood free me from all my sins and from every evil. Keep me faithful to your teaching, and never let me be parted from you.

> *or*

> Lord Jesus Christ, with faith in your love and mercy I eat your body and drink your blood. Let it not bring me condemnation, but health in mind and body.

He continues aloud:

> This is the Lamb of God
> who takes away the sins of the world.
> Happy are those who are called to his supper.
> **Lord I am not worthy to receive you,**
> **but only say the word and I shall be healed.**

THE COMMUNION

During the distribution of Communion a hymn may be sung.
If there is no hymn the Communion Antiphon is recited.

We become ever more closely one with Christ and with each
other by sharing in the 'one bread', receiving together the body
and blood of Jesus Christ in Holy Communion. Each one of
us should do everything possible to receive communion at
every Mass we share.

As the priest or minister offers the host (and the chalice) to
each person he says:

> The body [or blood] of Christ.

The Communicant replies:

> **Amen.**

After communion a period of silence is observed.
A thanksgiving hymn may be sung.

After Holy Communion, rather than wanting the Mass to end
quickly, we should be happy to spend a few minutes silently
enjoying Christ's presence in us. Here we need say nothing,
or only 'Jesus'. We can rest in his love, in peace and joy.

PRAYER AFTER COMMUNION

To end the Communion Rite the priest reads the Prayer after
Communion, in which in the name of the whole assembly he
gives thanks to God for the great gifts received.

THE CONCLUDING RITE

Brief announcements may be made.

Finally the priest blesses the congregation and then, the mass
over, he invites everyone to leave ready 'to love and serve the
Lord'.

> The Lord be with you. **And also with you.**
>
> May Almighty God bless you, the Father, the Son,
> and the Holy Spirit. **Amen.**

On special occasions the blessing may take a more solemn
form:

> Go in the peace of Christ.
>
> *or*
>
> The Mass is ended, go in peace.
>
> *or*
>
> Go in peace to love and serve the Lord.
> **Thanks be to God.**

We have worshipped together in the Eucharist. When Mass is
ended we should go out joyfully to the world, continuing to
greet each other in joy and service, for we go as Christ's
messengers to the world he has made in which we live.

Some prayers of thanksgiving can be found in the earlier
section of traditional prayers.

Devotion to the Blessed Sacrament

After the priest and people have shared in worshipping God through the Eucharistic Sacrifice and Holy Communion at Mass, it is customary to keep the remaining Consecrated Hosts (the Body and Blood of Jesus Christ under the appearance of bread, called the Blessed Sacrament) in the tabernacle on or near the altar in church. From this tabernacle, the sick and housebound can share the Eucharist they could not attend, by a priest, religious or commissioned lay person bringing Holy Communion to their homes.

But the Blessed Sacrament also forms a focal point for public and private devotion in church.

A good habit to develop is that of popping into the Church often during the week, to spend a little time quietly, at peace, openly before the Lord present in the Blessed Sacrament. Young and old, whoever we are, whatever is happening in our lives it is good to come in prayer before the lord in this way.

We can share our joys, our worries, our hopes and our fears with him. We can all find depth, refreshment and a new serenity if we allow some time for God, sitting or kneeling, saying prayers silently, perhaps simply repeating: God loves me.

HOLY HOUR – EXPOSITION

A long-standing, traditional series of devotions surround the exposing of the Blessed Sacrament on the altar. Exposition helps us because humanly-spiritually we are aided by a 'focal point', a centre for our attention.

Though a Holy Hour may be planned into singing, praying, silence and Benediction, development in prayer may lead us to greater silent attention. We should not be afraid to place ourselves in the presence of Jesus in the Blessed Sacrament and to remain there silently for an hour. Doing what? Being in the presence of the Lord.

BENEDICTION

This is a beautiful service, which can be lengthened or shortened according to the occasion and the mood of those taking part in the exposition of the Blessed Sacrament with hymns, prayers and the blessing.

For a very long time it was the normal evening service, especially on a Sunday, and was preceded often by the Rosary and a sermon.

The traditional form of simple Benediction is given here, with the ancient hymns and prayers.

Today, it is probably useful when there are longer pauses for silence, when hymns are varied, when the internal or surrounding devotions are more widely drawn. For instance, in Lent, one or more Stations of the Cross may be meditated, with a brief explanation and a period of silent, absorbing contemplation. A very lovely, prayerful and peaceful form of worship can be a mixture of evening prayer, or compline (some two or three psalms, etc), joined to Benediction.

As the minister comes to open the tabernacle one of the following, or some other Eucharistic hymn or chant may be sung:

Adoramus te Domine

Taizé 11 - Celebration Hymnal for Everyone

Be still for the presence of the lord

72 - Celebration Hymnal for Everyone

O saving victim, opening wide
the gate of heaven to man below;
our foes press on from every side;
your aid supply, your strength bestow.

To your great name be endless praise,
immortal Godhead, one in three;
O grant us endless length of days
in our true native land with thee. Amen.

or

O salutaris hostia,
quae caeli pandis ostium;
bella premunt hostilia,
da robur, fer auxilium.

Uni Trinoque Domino
sit sempiterna gloria,
qui vitam sine termino
nobis donet in patria.
Amen.

Then follow suitable hymns, prayers, readings and times for silent prayers.

Then everybody sings this hymn:

> Therefore we, before him bending,
> this great Sacrament revere;
> types and shadows have their ending,
> for the newer rite is here;
> faith our outward sense befriending,
> makes the inward vision clear.
>
> Glory let us give, and blessing
> to the Father and the Son;
> honour, might, and praise addressing,
> while eternal ages run;
> ever too his love confessing,
> who, from both, with both is one.
> Amen.

> *or*

> Tantum ergo Sacramentum
> veneremur cernui:
> et antiquum documentum
> novo cedat ritui:
> praestet fides supplementum
> sensuum defectui.
>
> Genitori, genitoque
> laus et jubilatio.
> Salus, honor, virtus quoque
> sit et benedictio;
> procedenti ab utroque
> compar sit laudatio.
> Amen.

You have given your people bread from heaven.
(Alleluia).
The bread which is full of all goodness. (Alleluia).

Let us pray: Lord Jesus Christ,
you gave us the eucharist
as the memorial of your suffering and death.
May our worship of this sacrament of your body and
    blood
help us to experience the salvation you won for us
and the peace of the kingdom
where you live with the Father and the Holy Spirit,
one God, for ever and ever. **Amen.**

or Panem de caelo praestitisti eis. (Alleluia).
Omne delectamentum in se habentem. (Alleluia).

Oremus. Deus, qui nobis, sub Sacramento mirabili,
passionis tuae memoriam reliquisti: tribue, quaesumus;
ita nos Corporis et Sanguinis tui sacra mysteria
venerari, ut redemptionis tuae fructum in nobis jugiter
sentiamus: qui vivis et regnas in saecula saeculorum.
Amen.

Now, bowing down in adoration, receive the blessing.

While the priest replaces the Blessed Sacrament in the
tabernacle, the following Psalm may be sung:

Let us adore for ever the most holy Sacrament.
O praise the Lord, all you nations;
praise him, all you people.
For his mercy is confirmed upon us;
and the truth of the Lord remains for ever.
Glory be to the Father, and to the Son,
and to the Holy Spirit.

As it was in the beginning, is now,
and ever shall be, world without end.
Amen.

Let us adore for ever the most holy Sacrament.

or

Adoremus in aeternum sanctissiumum Sacramentum.

Laudate Dominum, omnes gentes;
laudate eum omnes populi.

Quoniam confirmata est super nos misericordia ejus;
et veritas Domini manet in aeternum.

Gloria Patri, et Filio,
et Spiritui Sancto.

Sicut erat in principio, et nunc, et semper,
et in saecula saeculorum. Amen.

Adoremus in aeternum sanctissimum Sacramentum.

Prayer for Christian unity

O Lord Jesus Christ, when you were about to suffer, you
prayed for your disciples to the end of time, that they might
all be one, as you are in the Father, and the Father in you.
Look down in pity on the many divisions among those
who profess your faith, and heal the wounds which the
pride of man and the craft of Satan have inflicted on your
people. Break down the walls of separation which divide
one part and denomination of Christians from another.
Look with compassion on the souls who have been born
in one or another of these various communions and bring
them all into that one communion which you set up in the
beginning, the one, holy, catholic and apostolic Church.

THE LORD HAS DONE GREAT THINGS FOR ME

HOLY IS HIS NAME

The Sacramental Life of the Church

The church accepts seven sacraments. They are not unlike Shakespeare's seven ages of man. Sacraments are made for man, not man for the sacraments. This old saying puts the right emphasis. Each sacrament in its proper place and time has a real strength and growth to give to the individual who accepts the gift of God.

BAPTISM

A child or adult becomes part of the body of Christ by baptism, a member of a community, having a new relationship with God and mankind. This relationship should continue to grow, and each of us is personally responsible.

We make promises or they are made for us. But each must live out the promise according to his or her capacity to be open to the work of God's spirit. The following prayers from the Rite of Baptism may help to remind and renew our dedication.

The priest says to the parents:

> You have asked to have your children baptised. In doing
> so you are accepting the responsibility of training them
> in the practice of the faith. It will be your duty to bring
> them up to keep God's commandments as Christ taught
> us, by loving God and our neighbour. Do you clearly un-
> derstand what you are undertaking?

The parents answer:
We do.

The priest says to the godparents:

> Are you ready to help these parents in their duty as Chris-
> tian mothers and fathers?

They answer:
We are.

After the parents have professed their faith and the child has
been baptised, a lighted candle is given to the parent or
godparent, and the priest continues:

> Receive the light of Christ. Parents and godparents, this
> light is entrusted to you to be kept burning brightly. These
> children of yours have been enlightened by Christ. They
> are to walk always as children of the light. May they keep
> the flame of faith alive in their hearts. When the Lord
> comes, may they go out to meet him with all the saints in
> the heavenly kingdom.

At the beautiful first Easter ceremony on Holy Saturday, the
church reminds us of the light of Christ, and asks us to join in
renewing our own baptismal promises. Do we do this?

HOLY COMMUNION
(See Mass and Devotion to the Blessed Sacrament)

The desire of Jesus, strongly expressed again in recent instructions of the church, is that we frequently receive Holy Communion, and from quite an early age. We should each develop the 'habit' of receiving communion at Mass as a natural fulfilment of loving worship.

When bringing up young children, it is helpful to bring them to the altar even before they are ready to receive communion, to receive a blessing. When children begin to come to communion, the example and sharing of the parents is very important.

PENANCE OR CONFESSION

There has been a long and varied history of confession of sins. In very early days, it was once in a lifetime, later it became more and more frequent, to a weekly or sometimes daily routine. Recently, there has been some return to a more spaced confession.

A new rite of penance has been introduced since Vatican II. It is worth trying to get a little booklet on it. Look also at the section on the Mass (p25)

Penance is a 'public' sacrament, in that it has to do with our failure in relation to God and our fellow men and women, and the world in general.

Not all failure and wrong-doing needs the sacrament, because we can turn to God ourselves, declare our sorrow and in sorrow and joy receive communion. But sometimes we are so selfish and destructive in what we say or do, or fail to do, that we break off our relationship with God. Then we need to restore this, not only within ourselves, but 'publicly' by asking the priest for absolution and so reconciling ourselves with Christ and his church.

It is also spiritually wholesome and growthful to put ourselves humbly before the church (in the person of the priest) and Christ in confession regularly, but not necessarily very frequently. Some like a week, some a month, some three months. The church urges once a year at least.

Confession used normally to be in a confessional. More recently the practice of confession in a room, face to face has increased. This is useful in helping priest and penitent to go forward in Christ: it is simpler to give help and direction face to face.

An examination of conscience

Everything is summed up in the two great commandments: LOVE GOD; LOVE YOUR NEIGHBOUR (AS YOURSELF). Some like to use the ten commandments as aids. These suggestions are perhaps different. All sin begins with SELFISHNES...

God

   Do I choose myself before God?
   Do I neglect prayer time?
   Do I neglect Mass?
   Do I seek his will?
   Do I spread his word?
   Do I show his love and care in my life and actions?
   Do I deny him, doubt him, blaspheme against him?
   Do I live like Christ in poverty, accept rejection?
   Do I fast and do penance?
   Do I love him?

Neighbour

Do I know my neighbour… or want to know him?
Do I seek out the poor and help them?
Am I concerned about the Third World, starvation?
Do I visit the sick, those in prison?
Do I take part in groups or parish activities?
Am I concerned about local or national politics, laws
    on abortion or euthanasia, racial discrimination,
    housing, and so on?
Do I help young people in clubs, groups etc?
Do I help the old and lonely?
Do I respect my neighbour – property, good name?
Do I love my neighbour properly – affection, love, sex?
Do I love God's world and help to look after
    the environment?

Myself

Do I give God enough of myself?
Do I give time to think out where I am going?
Do I try to learn more about God by reading, groups,
listening to talks, discussions?
Do I discipline myself in my sexual habits,
    in eating and drinking, smoking all self-indulgence?
Do I listen?
Do I give in to pride – lying, anger, and so on?

These thoughts are just to stir you. Sit openly and think/pray
your life through, your relationship with God, with nature,
with people. Admit your failings before God.

CONFIRMATION

The Holy Spirit is vital to each of us. Yet we can easily forget him and his presence in us. Today there is a greater sense of his power at work in the church and people of the world. Giving us new life in Baptism, the Holy Spirit strengthens us in Confirmation.

Those who have been confirmed should remember daily their pledge to go out into the world to witness to Christ, and renew it. Remember, too, the words of the Bishop as he laid his hand on you and made the sign of the cross on your forehead with Chrism:

'Be sealed with the Gift of the Holy Spirit'.

Frequently call upon the Spirit in your life, with praise and thanksgiving, asking Him to fill you with his gifts.

PRIESTHOOD

By the laying on of hands by the Bishop, and the gift of God, a man is ordained to minister to God to his creation in preaching the Word and other ways but, especially and uniquely in celebrating the Eucharist.

Bishops, priests and deacons daily stand in need of prayer from all people. Prayer too is needed that God may inspire more to come forward in his priestly service.

If YOU are single and male of any age, God may be calling you. Impossible… not ME! However, unlikely, try being still, listening to Him, and asking. Then talk to a priest about the possibility.

Given the call and blessing of God, vocation to priesthood, which is a mysterious adventure is a life full of variety, challenge, pain, love and joy.

More recently, the church has also admitted the making of permanent deacons, both single and married.

MARRIAGE – AND FAMILY LIFE

This sacrament has such an important place in the life of so many men, women and children, and in society as a whole that it needs a careful, open and loving approach. There is so much to learn of oneself and the other, so much depends upon right choice and a right attitude. The mutual totality of giving, the trust and love, and the acceptance of God's grace to support us on every day of married and family life – all these make demands.

Husband and wife will find strength, comfort and joy in renewing their marriage vows together each anniversary.

If there are any difficulties which seem insoluble, prayer is very important. But it may still be necessary and important to seek together the advice of a skilled counsellor.

The Catholic Marriage Advisory Council has many local branches. Information can be obtained from your parish or from the CMAC headquarters: Clitherow House, 1 Blythe Mews, Blythe Road, London W14 0NW. Tel: 0171 371 1341. They also arrange good marriage preparation courses.

Sickness and Death

Sometime or other, one of your friends or relatives will be ill or even die. Do not be afraid to visit a sick or dying person or to see a dead body. Try to face death with its sadness and tears and loss and emptiness. If we believe in Jesus, we accept that we all die, in order to go to be with Jesus and to meet again all those we know and love... in heaven, in joy. But when a person is sick or old, he or she needs lots of care and love. They can be very lonely. Why not try to visit a sick or old person. Chat to them, laugh with them, cry with them... and do a little to help them. They need things done, they need company, they love young people. For you it may sometimes be a 'bore... for them it is joy... and if you visit them, you may well come to enjoy it too.

ANOINTING OF THE SICK AND DYING

The apostle James writes: "If any one of you is ill, he should send for the priest of the church and they must anoint him with oil in the name of the Lord, and pray over him. The prayer of faith will save the sick man and the Lord will raise him up again, and if he has committed any sins, he will be forgiven." You can be anointed at any time you are sick and churches often have healing services. Some anointing is a simple blessing and prayer for healing, and may be done by anyone. The sacrament of the anointing of the sick is given by a priest using oil specially blessed for this purpose.

PRAYING FOR OTHERS WHEN THEY ARE SICK

Lord, the one that I love is sick and in great pain; out of your compassion heal him and take away his pain. It breaks my heart to see him suffer; may I not share his pain if it is not your will that he be healed? Lord, let him know that you are with him: support and help him that he may come to know you more deeply as a result of his suffering. Lord be our strength and support in this time of darkness and give us that deep peace which comes from trusting you.

God of love,
ever caring
ever strong,
stand by us in our time of need.

Watch over *N.* who is sick,
look after him/her in every danger,
and grant him/her your healing and peace.
We ask this in the name of Jesus the Lord.

Father,
in your love you gave us Jesus
to help us rise triumphant over grief and pain.
Look on your child *N.* who is sick
and see in his/her sufferings those of Jesus your Son.

Grant *N.* a share in the strength you granted your Son
that he/she too may be a sign
of your goodness, kindness and loving care.
We ask this in the name of Jesus the Lord.

Lord Jesus Christ, our Redeemer,
by the grace of your Holy Spirit
cure the weakness of your servant *N.*

Heal his/her sickness and forgive his/her sins;
expel all afflications of mind and body;
mercifully restore him/her to full health,
and enable him/her to resume his/her former duties,
for you are Lord for ever and ever. Amen.

PRAYERS FOR TIMES WHEN YOU ARE SICK YOURSELF

O God make me brave,
let me strengthen after pain
as a tree strengthens after rain, shining and lovely
again.
As the blown grass lifts, let me rise
from sorrow with wise eyes,
knowing Thy way is wise.

God patient and kind,
I am ill and I find it difficult to be ill.
I keep saying things I don't mean,

I make life hard for those around me,
who are caring for me.
I don't find it easy to say that I'm sorry
when I know I've made them cross
or hurt them.
Please help me
to be patient with myself
and patient with others.
And, Lord, if I say the wrong thing,
or if I get impatient,
pour out your blessings on
my family and friends
heal the hurt
and help us grow strong in love
for each other and for you.
Amen.

Psalm 91

Those the dwell in the shelter of the Most High
and abide in the shade of the almighty
say to the Lord: "My refuge,
my stronghold, my God in whom I trust!"

It is God who will free you
from the snare of the fowler who seeks to destroy
you;
God will conceal you with his pinions
and under his wings you will find refuge.

You will not fear the terror of the night,
nor the arrow that flies by day,
nor the plague that prowls in the darkness
nor the scourge that lays waste at noon.

A thousand may fall at your side,
ten thousand fall at your right,
you it will never approach;
God's faithfulness is buckler and shield.

Your eyes have only to look,
to see how the wicked are repaid,
you who have said: "Lord, my refuge!"
and have made the Most High your dwelling.

Upon you no evil shall fall,
no plague approach where you dwell.
For you God has commanded the angels,
to keep you in all your ways.

They shall bear you upon their hands
lest you strike your foot against a stone.
On the lion and the viper you will tread
and trample the young lion and the dragon.

You set your love on me so I will save you,
protect you for you know my name.
When I call I shall answer: "I am with you."
I will save you in distress and give you glory.

With length of life I will content you;
I shall let you see my saving power.

Matthew 11:28-30

Come to me, all who labour and are heavy laden, and I will give you rest.

Take my yoke upon you, and learn from me; for I am gentle and lowly in heart, and you will find rest for your souls.

For my yoke is easy, and my burden is light.

2 Corinthians 1:3-5

Blessed be the God and Father of our Lord Jesus Christ, the Father of mercies and God of all comfort, who comforts us in all our affliction, so that we may be able to comfort those who are in any affliction, with the comfort with which we ourselves are comforted by God.

For as we share abundantly in Christ's sufferings, so through Christ we share abundantly in comfort too.

Jesus, Mary and Joseph, I give you my heart and my soul.

Jesus, Mary and Joseph, assist me in my last agony.

Jesus, Mary and Joseph, may I breathe forth my soul in peace with you.

Prayers for those who have recently died

> Almighty and eternal God
> hear our prayers for *N.*
> whom you have called from this life to yourself.
> Grant him/her light, happiness and peace.
>
> Let him/her pass in safety through the gates of death,
> and live for ever with all your saints
> in the light you promised to Abraham
> and to all his descendents in faith.
>
> Guard him/her from all harm
> and on that great day of resurrection and reward
> raise him/her up with all your saints.
> Pardon his/her sins
> and give him/her eternal life in your kingdom.
> We ask this through Christ our Lord

Prayers for a child who has died

> To you, O Lord,
> we humbly entrust *N.*
> so precious in your sight.
> Take him/her into your arms
> and welcome him/her into paradise,
> where there will be no sorrow, no weeping, nor pain,
> but the fullness of peace and joy
> with your Son and the Holy Spirit
> for ever and ever. Amen.

Destroy this temple and in three days I will raise it up

The Stations of the Cross

IT IS said the early pilgrims to Jerusalem and the crusaders brought back this devotion from the pilgrimage round the streets of the Holy City. Each church or home becomes today's Jerusalem if we walk and pray the Stations. As we join Christ on his last journey our thoughts can be our own on the Passion or from the Gospel story or a suggested text, like the one below.

It is good sometimes to join others, sometimes to pray alone. One single station may prove enough one day – on another all fourteen. You can add other 'incidents', especially the Resurrection.

One way of praying the Stations is to look at each Station, kneel and say:

We adore you, O Christ, and we bless you.
Because by your holy cross you have redeemed the world.

Then stand and think and pray the message of the Station.

FIRST STATION   **Jesus is condemned to death**

Our Journey in prayer begins as Jesus' journeys come to an end. He has travelled far and wide offering people healing and forgiveness, calling them to new life, to live the life of the Kingdom. Now he stands bound, condemned to die on the cross. Yet while others might see this as an opportunity for despair he sees it as a further opportunity for faith.

Lord by your cross and resurrection you have set us free. You are the saviour of the world.

SECOND STATION   **Jesus takes up his cross**

Jesus told his disciples - if anyone would follow me, let them take up their cross and follow me. As we remember Jesus carrying his cross, let us call to mind the cross we carry. Crosses of pain and sickness? The Cross of having to spend more time than we would like caring for someone? The Cross of being the 'odd one out' because of our faith, and wanting to live that faith like Jesus did?

Lord by your cross and resurrection you have set us free. You are the saviour of the world.

THIRD STATION — Jesus falls for the first time

It is humiliating not to be as strong as we would like. No sooner has Jesus started this last journey than his weakness is displayed for all to see. Sprawled on the ground just like anyone else. As we understand his weakness, so he understands ours.

Lord by your cross and resurrection you have set us free. You are the saviour of the world.

FOURTH STATION — Jesus meets his mother

To see someone you love suffering is always hard to bear. And so often you can do nothing to take the suffering away. This is Jesus' experience at this time, and his mother's too. Yet she is there, with her son, staying with him in his pain and humiliation, in his dying - because she loves him. How could she want to be anywhere else?

Lord by your cross and resurrection you have set us free. You are the saviour of the world.

FIFTH STATION   Simon helps Jesus carry his cross

Simon is called out of the crowd
to bear the cross. Probably not
something he expected to be asked
to do. But Simon does it, and does
it in love. There are many
opportunities for us to do the same
thing - to share another's burden.
Sometimes we can plan things like
this in advance. But how do we
react when we are asked to help at
a moment's notice

**Lord by your cross and resurrection you have set us free.
You are the saviour of the world.**

SIXTH STATION   Veronica wipes the face of Jesus

Veronica steps forward to wipe the
sweat and blood from Jesus' face.
The image of his face remains on
her cloth. Jesus tells us that when
we feed the hungry or care for the
sick we feed and care for him. Do
we see the face of the Lord in
others? Can we go to them in
love?

**Lord by your cross and resurrection you have set us free.
You are the saviour of the world.**

SEVENTH STATION   Jesus falls the second time

The journey in long. It is hard.
And for what? The surprising
thing is not that Jesus falls again,
but that he struggles to get up. He
struggles to be true to what he
believes in - to witness to the
power and love of God.

**Lord by your cross and resurrection you have set us free.
You are the saviour of the world.**

EIGHTH STATION
Jesus meets the women of Jerusalem

The women weep for Jesus, but
he warns them that there are
others who are in greater need
of compassion - all those who
turn from the Lord, and refuse
to see what he is offering them
and asking of them. Can we
have similar compassion for
those who are hard of heart?

**Lord by your cross and resurrection you have set us free.
You are the saviour of the world.**

NINTH STATION   Jesus falls for the third time

Is there no end to the suffering? Exhausted, Jesus collapses. He has reached the place of his execution. He has nothing now to do, but he has much still to endure.

Lord by your cross and resurrection you have set us free. You are the saviour of the world.

TENTH STATION   Jesus is stripped of his garments

There is no end to the humiliation that the soldiers make Jesus endure. They strip him of his clothes trying to strip him of his dignity. In the garden of Eden Adam was ashamed of his nakedness and hid from God. Yet on Golgotha Jesus does not hide. His confidence in his Father's love is complete.

Lord by your cross and resurrection you have set us free. You are the saviour of the world.

ELEVENTH STATION   Jesus is nailed to the cross

Jesus hands and feet are nailed to
the cross. His passion is near its
end, but the dying is long and
painful. But in his heart there is no
hatred for those who cause him
such suffering. "Father, forgive
them, they do not know what they
are doing."

**Lord by your cross and resurrection you have set us free.
You are the saviour of the world.**

TWELFTH STATION   Jesus dies on the cross

The struggle is over, Jesus takes
his last breath and surrenders his
life. "Father into your hands I
commend my spirit."

**Lord by your cross and resurrection you
have set us free.You are the saviour of the
world.**

THIRTEENTH STATION
Jesus is taken down from the cross

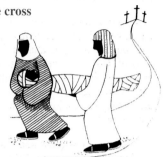

Jesus' body is lifted from the
wood of the cross. His mother
takes the body of her son in
her arms and weeps for love
of him.

**Lord by your cross and
resurrection you have set us
free. You are the saviour of
the world.**

FOURTEENTH STATION Jesus is laid in the tomb

Joseph of Arimethea takes the
body of Jesus and places it in his
own tomb. It must have seemed
that all was now finished, that
what ever hopes people had in
Jesus have died with him on the
cross. At the beginning of our
journey there was the choice to
despair or to have faith. It is the
same now.
Death is not the end. There is one
thing greater than death and that is
love. And God is love.

**Lord by your cross and resurrection you have set us free.
You are the saviour of the world.**

FIFTEENTH STATION   Jesus rises from the dead

Early in the morning the disciples come and find the tomb
empty. Mary of Magdalene remains, weeping. Jesus comes to
her, and ask why she weeps. Her tears of sadness turn to tears
of joy. May the joy of the resurrection live in our hearts, turn
our tears into laughter. May we like Mary carry in our hearts
and on our lips the good news that Jesus is risen from the
dead. He has conquered death and his kingdom of peace and
love will last for ever.

**Lord by your cross and resurrection you have set us free.
You are the saviour of the world.**

When praying the stations in a group it is common to sing a chant or a verse of a hymn, or say prayers, while walking from one station to another.

Suitable chants include:

> Behold the Lamb of God,
> behold the Lamb of God.
> He takes away the sin,
> the sin of the world.

or perhaps sing quietly these verses from '*Were you there when they crucified my lord?*'

After Stations 1–10

> Were you there when they crucified my Lord?
> Were you there when they crucified my Lord?
> Oh sometimes it causes me to tremble, tremble, tremble.
> Were you there when they crucified my Lord?

After Station 11

> Were you there when they nailed him to a tree? ...

After Station 12

> Were you there when the sun refused to shine? ...

After Station 13

> Were you there when they took him from the tree? ...

After Station 14

> Were you there when they laid him in the tomb? ...

After Station 15

> Were you there when he rose out of the tomb? ...

another suitable hymn:

> I met you at the cross,
> Jesus my Lord;
> I heard you from that cross:
> my name you called –
> asked me to follow you all of my days,
> asked me for evermore your name to praise.
>
> I saw you on the cross
> dying for me;
> I put you on that cross:
> but your one plea –
> would I now follow you all of my days
> and would I evermore your great name praise?
>
> Jesus, my Lord and King,
> Saviour of all,
> Jesus the King of kings,
> you heard my call –
> that I would follow you all of my days,
> and that for evermore your name I'd praise.

Eric A. Thorn
279 – Celebration Hymn for Everyone

When reciting prayers between the stations a common pattern
would be:

> Our Father,
> Hail Mary,
> Glory Be.

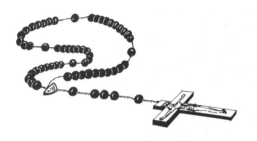

The Rosary

This well-tried and ancient devotion is so simple and effective, it should be known to all and loved by many.

The repetition of three basic prayers *Our Father*, *Hail Mary* and *Glory be to the Father* makes a rhythm which stills the person, occupies part of the mind and leaves one free to grow in meditation and contemplation.

Each person might well carry a rosary (either beads or a small wheel-rosary) and use it wholly or in part throughout the day.

The touch is important, and makes a prayer-memento. One or two *Our Fathers* or *Hail Marys* may be said anywhere, any time.

The layout of one *Our Father*, ten *Hail Marys* and one *Glory be to the Father* need not be used rigidly. But the suggested method is that each group or decade gives opportunity for thought on part or parts of the story of Jesus Christ and his Mother Mary. But just the words may be used, or one thought may fill all the decades. Other incidents in Christ's life could also be used.

THE JOYFUL MYSTERIES

Any of the happy events in the life of Jesus or Mary may be commemorated, such as the wedding at Cana, any of the healings, the calling of the Apostles, the teaching to pray, the sermon on the mount, the Last Supper and so on. But the traditional ones are as follows:

1. THE ANNUNCIATION

    The angel comes to Mary. The blessedness of Mary is that she said 'Yes' to God's request. Do I/we say 'Yes'?
    (Luke 1:26-38)

Thoughts: Wonder; joy; acceptance; listening; doing.

2. THE VISITATION

    Mary goes to her cousin Elizabeth. Her love and care is rewarded by Elizabeth's welcome and Mary responds with *the Magnificat*. Do we do out to others in joy and love? Do we proclaim the greatness of the Lord?
    (Luke 1:19-56)

Thoughts: Reaction to others; meeting Christ in others; wonder of God; humility; small is beautiful.

3. THE NATIVITY

    Jesus is born… God really lives among us. The world and human beings can never be quite the same again. Do we sit in contemplation of this 'happening'? Can we try to realise what it means to mankind?
    (Luke 21:1-20)

Thoughts: The sacredness and beauty of life in a child; the humility of God in Christ; he is really man; closeness of God and man/Christ/Mary/me.

4. THE PRESENTATION IN THE TEMPLE

Mary and Joseph fulfil the rules, Jesus is recognised by 'the church' (Simeon). Life is completed in 'meeting Jesus'. How do we react to 'the Law'? Do we recognise Jesus? Are we ready and happy to die?
(Luke 2:22-35)

Thoughts: Baptism – parents' attitude, adults' fulfilment. Who have I met today… and how? Can I say and mean the *Nunc Dimittis*?

5. THE FINDING OF JESUS IN THE TEMPLE

Jesus is apparently 'disobedient' to his parents. They find him after being anxious at losing him. He is 'about his father's business'. What is obedience? To whom? What is Our Father's business? Are we about it?
(Luke 2:41-52)

Thoughts: Do we listen and ask questions? Do we 'store things up' in our hearts? Do we 'grow in wisdom and grace'?

THE SORROWFUL MYSTERIES

Any of the sad happenings, like the joyful can be commemorated… the refusal at the Inn, the flight to Egypt, the massacre, the driving of Christ from Nazareth, the rejection at many points, the ingratitude of lepers and others… and so on. The traditional mysteries are:

1. THE AGONY IN THE GARDEN

While his disciples sleep, Jesus prays. The weight of fear and foreboding drain him, tax his trust in his father, beat him to the ground in utter acceptance of his Father's will. How do we react to fear and foreboding? Can we say: 'Thy will be done'? Do we believe Jesus really suffered?

(Luke 22:39-44)

Thoughts: do we pray or sleep? Being in agony he prayed the longer... do we?

2. THE SCOURGING AT THE PILLAR

Pilate was fed up with decision making, and scared. He washed his hands of Christ... and thought he would get rid of his problem by flogging him. Part of man wants to be free of Christ, part to be one with him. Part of man wants to please at all costs, and to keep in with authority.

(Luke 23:13-25)

Thoughts: Whose side are we on? Would we, do we wash our hands, or shout: 'Crucify him'?

3. THE CROWNING WITH THORNS

Was this a soldiers' game? Playing with Christ as they gambled, taunting him and mocking him after Pilate's questioning, and the scourging. A crowning insult after all the rest. Bringing out the almost thoughtless cruelty in human nature against a fallen fellow man.

(Matthew 27:27-31)

Thoughts: do we mock Christ unthinkingly by claiming but not living Christianity? Do we get at people weaker or sadder than ourselves? Are we kind... a mystic said 'Be kind, be kind and you will be a saint'.

4. THE CARRYING OF THE CROSS BY JESUS

Not only did Jesus submit to carrying the Cross on which he was to hang, he also accepted help in doing so. He emptied himself, was completely human and defenceless. He showed us an example. He did not give up.
(Matthew 27:32-38)

Thoughts: How easily do we give up? How do we take unjust dealings with us? Are we prepared to shoulder a particularly heavy weight or burden of our own or someone else's?

5. THE CRUCIFIXION AND DEATH OF JESUS

They did the ordinary, cruel law... they stuck nails into his hands and feet, raised him on a cross, and left him to die of pain, exposure, asphyxiation or shock. He submitted, he died... he really died. He faced this 'extinction', giving himself in trust to his Father.
(Matthew 27:39-50)

Thoughts: How cruel are we in 'the ordinary things' we do? Do we believe he really died? Do we think that, somehow, it was all right for him? Do we accept his darkness and abandonment?

THE GLORIOUS MYSTERIES

These cover all that happened after Christ rose from the dead. There are many things we could think about, including his appearances to the apostles, the growth of the early church, and all the history of the church down to today… glory mixed with joy and pain, so that all decades meet at this point.

1. THE RESURRECTION

   Placed in the tomb, according to the Scriptures, his body could not be found after three days. Instead, there was an empty tomb, and reports of Jesus being alive. Why look for the living among the dead. Here is an experience experienced and handed on, accepted by many.
   (Matthew 28; Mark 16; Luke 24; John 20)

   Thoughts: Do we believe with St Paul that if the Resurrection did not happen, then the preaching of the Gospel is in vain? Do we believe in after life? Are we prepared to die, and go to meet all those we love with the risen Lord in heaven?

2. THE ASCENSION

   The risen Jesus had finished his work in this world as man, and risen man, so he went back to his Father. His 'disappearance' was witnessed by believers (the apostles) who still doubted. It is not easy in a scientific age to accept Jesus 'going up to heaven', but it is a good way to picture his 'going'. It is still a matter of faith, and each of us is open to doubt.
   (Matthew 28:16-20; Acts 1:1-11)

   Thoughts: Is it possible that we should still 'doubt' while believing? Do we believe in heaven? Do we go on our way rejoicing?

3. THE COMING OF THE HOLY SPIRIT ON OUR LADY
   AND THE APOSTLES

   Gathered according to Christ's command, they received
   these fantastic gifts of the Spirit… love, joy, peace,
   patience, faith, courage. The effect was electric if not
   nuclear. A mind-shattering experience set of hundred of
   thousands of others. The tremors have been going on
   ever since. *(Acts 2:1-13)*

Thoughts: Have we received the Holy Spirit… and if so when?
Have we accepted him, and do we allow ourselves to be open to
his work in us?

4. THE ASSUMPTION

   There is no Scripture passage for this. We do not even
   know anything about the later life or death of Mary. But
   we may draw pointers from Scripture, and in 1950 Pope
   Pius XII declared the doctrine of the Assumption. It had
   been accepted and celebrated without definition in
   England at least since the days of King Alfred.
   (Revelation 12:1-6)

Thoughts: If Mary has been so uniquely close to Christ as his
Mother, must she not be in heaven with him? If blessedness is not
in begetting the child but in hearing the word of God and doing it',
should we not try to do the same?

5. THE CROWNING OF OUR LADY AS QUEEN OF HEAVEN

   Again… nothing in Scripture except as above. This may
   be a point at which the ordinary person saying the
   Rosary should sit still, not try to think, but try to absorb
   the glory – the immensity, the mystery, and the love of
   God… and to absorb that this, personalised in Mary, is
   for us, according to our 'hearing the word of God and
   doing it', here and now!

THE LITANY OF OUR LADY

Lord, have mercy	**Lord, have mercy.**
Christ, have mercy.	**Christ, have mercy.**
Lord, have mercy.	**Lord, have mercy.**
Christ, hear us.	**Christ, graciously hear us.**
God the Father of heaven,	**have mercy on us.**
God the Son, Redeemer of the world,	**have mercy on us.**
God the Holy Spirit, Holy Trinity, one God,	**have mercy on us.**
Holy Mary,	**pray for us.**
Holy Mother of God,	**pray for us.**
Holy Virgin of virgins,	**pray for us.**
Mother of Christ,	**pray for us.**
Mother of divine grace,	**pray for us.**
Mother most pure,	**pray for us.**
Mother most chaste,	**pray for us.**
Mother inviolate,	**pray for us.**
Mother undefiled,	**pray for us.**
Mother most lovable,	**pray for us.**
Mother most admirable,	**pray for us.**
Mother of good counsel,	**pray for us.**
Mother of our Creator,	**pray for us.**
Mother of our Saviour,	**pray for us.**
Virgin most prudent,	**pray for us.**
Virgin most venerable,	**pray for us.**
Virgin most renowned,	**pray for us.**
Virgin most powerful,	**pray for us.**
Virgin most merciful,	**pray for us.**
Virgin most faithful,	**pray for us.**
Mirror of justice,	**pray for us.**
Seat of wisdom,	**pray for us.**

Cause of our joy,	**pray for us.**
Spiritual vessel,	**pray for us.**
Vessel of honour,	**pray for us.**
Singular vessel of devotion,	**pray for us.**
Mystical rose,	**pray for us.**
Tower of David,	**pray for us.**
Tower of ivory,	**pray for us.**
House of God,	**pray for us.**
Ark of the covenant,	**pray for us.**
Gate of heaven,	**pray for us.**
Morning star,	**pray for us.**
Health of the sick,	**pray for us.**
Refuge of sinners,	**pray for us.**
Comfort of the afflicted,	**pray for us.**
Help of Christians,	**pray for us.**
Queen of Angels,	**pray for us.**
Queen of Patriarchs,	**pray for us.**
Queen of Prophets,	**pray for us.**
Queen of Apostles,	**pray for us.**
Queen of Martyrs,	**pray for us.**
Queen of Confessors,	**pray for us.**
Queen of Virgins,	**pray for us.**
Queen of all Saints,	**pray for us.**
Queen conceived without original sin,	**pray for us.**
Queen assumed into heaven,	**pray for us.**
Queen of the most holy Rosary,	**pray for us.**
Queen of peace,	**pray for us.**

Lamb of God, you take
away the sins of the world, **spare us, O Lord.**
Lamb of God, you take
away the sins of the world, **graciously hear us, O Lord.**

Lamb of God, you take
   away the sins of the world,   **have mercy on us.**
Pray for us, O holy Mother of God.
That we may be made worthy of the promises of Christ.

Let us pray: Grant that we your servants, Lord, may enjoy
unfailing health of mind and body, and through the prayers of
the ever blessed Virgin Mary in her glory, free us from our
sorrows in this world and give us eternal happiness in the next.
Through Christ our Lord. **Amen.**

THE MAGNIFICAT

My soul glorifies the Lord,
my spirit rejoices in God, my Saviour.
He looks on his servant in her nothingness;
henceforth all ages will call me blessed.
The Almighty works marvels for me.
Holy his name!
His mercy is from age to age,
on those who fear him.
He puts forth his arm in strength
and scatters the proud-hearted.
He casts the mighty from their throne
and raises the lowly.
He fills the starving with good things,
sends the rich away empty.
He protects Israel his servant,
remembering his mercy,
the mercy promised to our fathers,
for Abraham and his sons for ever.

Reading the Bible

THE Bible is not a book, it is a whole library. It contain lots of different books. In the same way that you could not read a whole library at once, so you could not read the Bible easily from cover to cover. It is easier for us to understand the huge area of the Books of the Bible, if we take it gently, dipping in.

First there are the books of the Old Testament. These are history, inspired folklore, myth, legend, poetry, prayer, law and administration, exploring work on God's nature and good and evil. There is prophecy and proverb. Through all these runs the revelation of God, the work of the Spirit.

Secondly there are the books of the New Testament which include the four differing accounts of the life of Jesus Christ, Son of God. These Gospels were written down quite a long time after Jesus was put to death and rose again. Before them in time were some of the other writings, and letters from St Paul and other apostles of varying dates to varying people. The New Testament also contains the Acts of the Apostles, a history of the early church.

The Bible is the chief source of revelation (that is God telling us about himself), it has also been preached down the ages, but is here gathered in written form. Every Catholic should be able to find a copy of the Bible to read and should read it regularly. But unless parents and teachers read the Bible, and evidently enjoy the reading, younger Catholics will not learn to read it.

There are many translations, some easier than others. Do not be afraid. The riches and beauty are tremendous. Some parts are deeply moving; there is a real gold-mine of prayer.

A few examples follow. Try if you can to read a little regularly, and listen well when you come to Mass, so that you can look up the passage at home, and discuss it with the family, or friends.

Before reading the Bible it is helpful to pray these verses from psalm 119 in preparation:

> Your word is a lamp for my steps
> and a light for my path.
> By your word give me life.

Conclude your time of reading and prayerful reflection with the following verses, also from psalm 119:

> Your word, O Lord, for ever
> stands firm in the heavens:
> your truth lasts from age to age
> like the earth you created.
>
> Glory be...

Genesis 1 and 2:1-4

In the beginning God created the heavens and the earth. Now the earth was a formless void, there was darkness over the deep, and God's spirit hovered over the water. God said: 'Let there be light', and there was light. God saw that light was good, and God divided light from darkness. God called light 'day', and darkness he called 'night'. Evening came and morning came: the first day.

God said: 'Let there be a vault in the waters to divide the waters in two'. And so it was. God made the vault, and it divided the waters above the vault from the waters under the vault. God called the vault 'heaven'. Evening came and morning came: the second day.

God said: 'Let the waters under heaven come together into a single mass, and let dry land appear'. And so it was. God called the dry land 'earth' and the mass of waters 'seas', and God saw that it was good.

God said: 'Let the earth produce vegetation: seed-bearing plants, and fruit trees bearing fruit with their seed inside, on the earth'. And so it was. The earth produced vegetation: plants bearing seed in their several kinds, and trees bearing fruit with their seed inside in their several kinds. God saw that it was good. Evening came and morning came: the third day.

God said: 'Let there be lights in the vault of heaven to divide day from night, and let them indicate festivals, days and years. Let there be lights in the vault of heaven to shine on the earth'. And so it was. God made the two great lights: the greater light to govern the day, the smaller light to govern the night, and the stars. God set them in the vault of heaven to shine on earth, to govern the day and the night and to divide light from darkness. God saw that it was good. Evening came and morning came: the fourth day.

God said: 'Let the waters teems with living creatures, and let birds fly above the earth within the vault of heaven'. And so it was. God created great sea-serpents and every kind of living creature with which the waters teem, and every kind of winged creature. God saw that it was good. God blessed them, saying: 'Be fruitful, multiply, and fill the waters of the seas: and let the birds multiply upon the earth'. Evening came and morning came: the fifth day.

God said: 'Let the earth produce every kind of living creature: cattle, reptiles, and every kind of wild beast'. And so it was. God made every kind of wild beast, every kind of land reptile. God saw that it was good.

God said: 'Let us make man in our own image, in the likeness of ourselves, and let them be masters of the fish of the sea, the birds of heaven, the cattle, all the wild beasts and all the reptiles that crawl upon the earth'.

God created man in the image of himself, in the image of God he created him, male and female he created them.

God blessed them, saying to them: 'Be fruitful, multiply, fill the earth and conquer it. Be masters of the fish of the sea, the birds of heaven and all living animals on the earth'.

God said: 'See, I give you all the seed-bearing plants that are upon the whole earth, and all the trees with seed-bearing fruit; this shall be your food. To all the wild beasts, all birds of heaven and all living reptiles on the earth I give all the foliage of plants for food'. And so it was. God saw all he had made, and indeed it was very good. Evening came and morning came: the sixth day.

Thus heaven and earth were completed with all their array. On the seventh day God completed the work he had been doing. God blessed the seventh day and made it holy, because on that day he has rested after all his work of creating. Such were the origins of heaven and earth when they were created.

Psalm 23

The Lord is my shepherd; there is nothing I shall want. Fresh and green are the pastures where he gives me repose. Near restful waters he leads me, to revive my drooping spirit.

He guides me along the right path; he is true to his name. If I should walk in the valley of darkness no evil would I fear. You are there with your crook and your staff; with these you give me comfort.

You have prepared a banquet for me in the sight of my foes. My head you have anointed with oil; my cup is over-flowing.

Surely goodness and kindness shall follow me all the days of my life. In the Lord's own house shall I dwell for ever and ever.

Psalm 100

> Cry out with joy to the Lord, all the earth.
> Serve the Lord with gladness.
> Come before him, singing for joy.
> Know that he, the Lord, is God.
> He made us, we belong to him.
> We are his people, the sheep of his flock.
> Go within his gates, giving thanks.
> Enter his courts with songs of praise.
> Give thanks to him and bless his name.
> Indeed, how good is the Lord,
> eternal his merciful love;
> he is faithful from age to age.

Isaiah 53

'Who could believe what we have heard, and to whom has the power of Yahweh been revealed?' Like a sapling he grew up in front of us, like a root in arid ground. Without beauty, without majesty (we saw him), no looks to attract our eyes; a thing despised and rejected by men, a man of sorrows and familiar with suffering, a man to make people screen their faces; he was despised and we took no account of him. And yet ours were the sufferings he bore, our the sorrows he carried. But we, thought of him as someone punished, struck by God, and brought low. Yet he was pierced through for our faults, crushed for our sins. On him lies a punishment that brings us peace, and through his wounds we are healed.

We had all gone astray like sheep, each taking his own way, and Yahweh burdened him with the sins of all of us. Harshly dealt with, he bore it humbly, he never opened his mouth, like a lamb that is led to the slaughter-house, like a sheep that is dumb before its shearers never opening its mouth.

By force and by law he was taken; would anyone plead his cause? Yes, he was torn away from the land of the living; for our faults struck down in death. They gave him a grave with the wicked, a tomb with the rich, though he had done no wrong and there had been no perjury in his mouth.

Yahweh has been pleased to crush him with suffering. If he offers his life in atonement, he shall see his heirs, he shall have a long life and through him what Yahweh wishes will be done.

His soul's anguish over, he shall see the light and be content. By his sufferings shall my servant justify many, taking their faults on himself.

Hence I will grant whole hordes for his tribute, he shall divide the spoil with the mighty, for surrendering himself to death and letting himself be taken for a sinner, while he was bearing the faults of many and praying all the time for sinners.

John 1:1-14

In the beginning was the Word: and the Word was with God: and the Word was God. The same was in the beginning with God.
All things were made by him: and without him was made nothing that was made. In him was life: and the life was the light of men. And the light shineth in darkness: and the darkness did not comprehend it.

There was a man sent from God, whose name was John. This man came for a witness, to give testimony of the light, that all men might believe through him.

He was not the light, but was to give witness to the light. That was the true light, which enlighteneth every man that cometh into this world. He was in the world: and the world was made by him: and the world knew him not.

He came unto his own: and his own received him not. But as many as received him, to them gave he the power to be made the sons of God, to them that believe in his name. Who are born, not of blood, nor of the will of the flesh, not of the will of man, but of God.

And the Word was made flesh, and dwelt among us (and we saw his glory, the glory as it were of the only begotten of the Father), full of grace and truth.

Luke 4: 16-19

He came to Nazareth, where he had been brought up, and went into the synagogue on the sabbath day as he usually did. He stood up to read, and they handed him the scroll of the prophet Isaiah. Unrolling the scroll he found the place where it is written:

> The spirit of the Lord has been given to me,
> for he has anointed me.
> He has sent me to bring the good news to the poor,
> to proclaim liberty to captives,
> and to the blind new sight,
> to set the downtrodden free,
> to proclaim the Lord's year of favour.

Acts 10: 34-36

Then Peter addressed them: 'The truth I have now come to realise', he said, 'is that God does not have favourites, but that anybody of any nationality who fears God and does what is right is acceptable to him.

'It is true, God sent his word to the people of Israel, and it was to them that the good news of peace was brought by Jesus Christ – Jesus Christ is Lord of all men.'

Matthew 5:1-12

Seeing the crowds, he went onto the mountain. And when he was seated his disciples came to him. Then he began to speak. This is what he taught them:
How blessed are the poor in spirit:
the kingdom of Heaven is theirs.
Blessed are the gentle:
they shall have the earth as inheritance.

Blessed are those who mourn:
they shall be comforted.
Blessed are those who hunger and thirst for uprightness:
they shall have their fill.
Blessed are the merciful:
they shall have mercy shown them.
Blessed are the pure in heart:
they shall see God.
Blessed are the peacemakers:
they shall be recognised as children of God.
Blessed are those who are persecuted in the cause of
uprightness:
the kingdom of Heaven is theirs.
Blessed are you when people abuse and persecute you and
speak all kinds of calumny against you falsely on my
account. Rejoice and be glad, for your reward will be great in
heaven; this is how they persecuted the prophets before you.

Luke 15:1-32

The tax collectors and sinners, however, were all crowding
round to listen to him, and the Pharisees and scribes com-
plained saying, 'This man welcomes sinners and eats with
them.' So he told them this parable:

'Which one of you with a hundred sheep, if he lost one,
would fail to leave the ninety-nine in the desert and go after
the missing one till he found it? And when he found it, would
he not joyfully take it on his shoulders and then, when he got
home, call together his friends and neighbours, saying to them,
"Rejoice with me, I have found my sheep that was lost." In
the same way, I tell you, there will be more rejoicing in heaven
over one sinner repenting than over ninety-nine upright people who have no need of repentance.

Or again, what woman with ten drachmas would not, if she lost one, light a lamp and sweep out the house and search thoroughly till she found it? And then, when she had found it, call together her friends and neighbours, saying to them, "Rejoice with me, I have found the drachma I lost." In the same way, I tell you, there is rejoicing among the angels of God over one repentant sinner.'

Then he said, 'There was a man who had two sons. The younger one said to his father, "Father, let me have the share of the estate that will come to me." So the father divided the property between them. A few days later, the younger son got together everything he had and left for a distant country where he squandered his money on a life of debauchery.

'When he had spent it all, that country experienced a severe famine, and now he began to feel the pinch; so he hired himself out to one of the local inhabitants who put him on his farm to feed the pigs. And he would willingly have filled himself with the husks the pigs were eating but no one would let him have them. Then he came to his senses and said, "How many of my father's hired men have all the food they want and more, and here am I dying of hunger! I will leave this place and go to my father and say: Father, I have sinned against heaven and against you; I no longer deserve to be called you son; treat me as one of your hired men." So he left the place and went back to his father.

'While he was still a long way off, his father saw him and was moved with pity. He ran to the boy, clasped him in his arms and kissed him. Then his son said, "Father, I have sinned against heaven and against you. I no longer deserve to be called you son." But the father said to his servants, "Quick! Bring out the best robe and put it on him; put a ring on his finger and sandals on his feet. Bring the calf we have been fattening, and kill it; we will celebrate by having a feast, because this son of mine was dead and has come back to life; he was lost and is found." And they began to celebrate.

'Now the elder son was out in the fields, and on his way back, as he drew near the house, he could hear music and dancing. Calling one of the servants he asked what it was all about. The servant told him, "Your brother has come, and your father has killed the calf we had been fattening because he has got him back safe and sound." He was angry then and refused to go in, and his father came out and began to urge him to come in; but he retorted to his father, "All these years I have slaved for you and never once disobeyed any orders of yours, yet you never offered me so much as a kid for me to celebrate with my friends. But, for this son of yours, when he comes back after swallowing up your property – he and his loose women - you kill the calf we had been fattening."

'The father said, "My son, you are with me always and all I have is yours. But it was only right we should celebrate and rejoice, because your brother here was dead and has come to life; he was lost and is found." '

John 8:2-11

At daybreak he appeared in the Temple again; and as all the people came to him, he sat down and began to teach them.

The scribes and Pharisees brought a woman along who had been caught committing adultery; and making her stand there in the middle they said to Jesus, 'Master, this woman was caught in the very act of committing adultery, and in the Law Moses has ordered us to stone women of this kind. What have you got to say?' They asked him this as a test, looking for an accusation to use against him. But Jesus bent down and started writing on the ground with his finger. As they persisted with their question, he straightened up and said, 'Let the one among you who is guiltless be the first to throw a stone at her.' Then he bent down and continued writing on the ground. When they heard this they went away one by one, beginning with the eldest, until the last one had gone and Jesus was left alone with the woman, who remained in the middle. Jesus again straightened up and said, 'Woman, where are they? Has no one condemned you?' 'No one, sir,' she replied. 'Neither do I condemn you,' said Jesus. 'Go away, and from this moment sin no more.'

Mark 10:46-52

They reached Jericho; and as he left Jericho with his disciples and a great crowd, Bartimaeus - that is, the son of Timaeus - a blind beggar, was sitting at the side of the road. When he heard that it was Jesus of Nazareth, he began to shout and cry out, 'Son of David, Jesus, have pity on me.' And many of them scolded him and told him to keep quiet, but he only shouted all the louder, 'Son of David, have pity on me.' Jesus stopped and said, 'Call him here.' So they called the blind man over. 'Courage,' they said, 'get up; he is calling you.' So throwing off his cloak, he jumped up and went to Jesus. Then Jesus spoke, 'What do you want me to do for you?' The blind man said to him, 'Rabbuni, let me see again.' Jesus said to him, 'Go; your faith has saved you.' And at once his sight returned and he followed him along the road.

Mark 15:25-39

It was the third hour when they crucified him. The inscription giving the charge against him read, 'The King of the Jews'. And they crucified two bandits with him, one on his right and one on his left.

The passers-by jeered at him; they shook their heads and said, 'Aha! So you would destroy the Temple and rebuild it in three days! Then save yourself; come down from the cross!' The chief priests and the scribes mocked him among themselves in the same way with the words, 'He saved others, he cannot save himself. Let the Christ, the king of Israel, come down from the cross now, for us to see it and believe.' Even those who were crucified with him taunted him.

When the sixth hour came there was darkness over the whole land until the ninth hour. And at the ninth hour Jesus cried out in a loud voice, *'Eloi, eloi, lama sabachthani?'* which means, *'My God, my God, why have you forsaken me?'* When some of those who stood by heard this, they said, 'Listen, he is calling on Elijah.' Someone ran and soaked a sponge in vinegar and, putting it on a reed, gave it to him to drink saying, 'Wait! And see if Elijah will come to take him down.' But Jesus gave a loud cry and breathed his last. And the veil of the Sanctuary was torn in two from top to bottom. The centurion, who was standing in front of him had seen how he had died, and he said, 'In truth this man was Son of God.'

John 20:1-18

It was very early on the first day of the week and still dark, when Mary of Magdala came to the tomb. She saw that the stone had been moved away from the tomb and came running to Simon Peter and the other disciple, the one whom Jesus loved. 'They have taken the Lord out of the tomb,' she said, 'and we don't know where they have put him.'

So Peter set out with the other disciple to go to the tomb. They ran together, but the other disciple, running faster than Peter, reached the tomb first; he bent down and saw the linen cloths lying on the ground, but did not go in. Simon Peter, following him, also came up, went into the tomb, saw the linen cloths lying on the ground and also the cloth that had been over his head; this was not with the linen cloths but rolled up in a place by itself. Then the other disciple who had reached the tomb first also went in; he saw and he believed. Till this moment they had still not understood the scripture, that he must rise from the dead. The disciples then went back home.

But Mary was standing outside near the tomb, weeping. Then, as she wept, she stooped to look inside, and saw two angels in white sitting where the body of Jesus had been, one at the head, the other at the feet. They said, 'Woman, why are you weeping?' 'They have taken my Lord away,' she replied, 'and I don't know where they have put him.' As she said this she turned round and saw Jesus standing there, though she did not realise that it was Jesus. Jesus said to her, 'Woman, why are you weeping? Who are you looking for?' Supposing him to be the gardener, she said, 'Sir, if you have taken him away, tell me where you have put him, and I will go and remove him.' Jesus said, 'Mary!' She turned round then and said to him in Hebrew, 'Rabboni!' – which means Master. Jesus said to her, 'Do not cling to me, because I have not yet ascended to the Father. But go to the brothers, and tell them: I am ascending to my Father and your Father, to my God and your God.' So Mary of Magdala told the disciples, 'I have seen the Lord,' and that he had said these things to her.

Romans 8:22-27

From the beginning till now the entire creation, as we know, has been groaning in one great act of giving birth; and not only creation, but all of us who possess the first-fruits of the Spirit, we too groan inwardly as we wait for our bodies to be set free. For we must be content to hope that we shall be saved

– our salvation is not in sight, we should not have to be hoping
for it if it were – but, as I say, we must hope to be saved since
we are not saved yet – it is something we must wait for with
patience.

The Spirit too comes to help us in our weakness. For when
we cannot choose words in order to pray properly, the Spirit
himself expresses our plea in a way that could never be put into
words, and God who knows everything in our hearts knows
perfectly well what he means, and that the pleas of the saints
expressed by the Spirit are according to the mind of God.

Ephesians 3:14-21

This, then, is what I pray, kneeling before the Father, from
whom every family, whether spiritual or natural, takes its name:
out of his infinite glory, may he give you the power through
his Spirit for your hidden self to grow strong, so that Christ
may live in your hearts through faith, and then, planted in
love and built on love, you will with all the saints have strength
to grasp the breadth and the length, the height and the depth;
until, knowing the love of Christ, which is beyond all
knowledge, you are filled with the utter fullness of God.

Glory be to him whose power, working in us, can do
infinitely more than we imagine; glory be to him from
generation to generation in the church and in Christ Jesus for
ever and ever. Amen.

James 1: 23-27

To listen to the word and not obey is like looking at your own
features in a mirror, and then, after a quick look, going off
and immediately forgetting what you looked like. But the man
who looks steadily at the perfect law of freedom and makes

that his habit – not listening and then forgetting, but actively putting it into practice – will be happy in all that he does.

Nobody must imagine that he is religious while he still goes on deceiving himself and not keeping control over his tongue; anyone who does this has the wrong idea of religion. Pure, unspoilt religion, in the eyes of God our Father is this: coming to the help of orphans and widows when they need it, and keeping oneself uncontaminated by the world.

Other passages come throughout this prayer book, and you should refer to them. It is good, in reading the Bible to read slowly, a little bit at a time, thinking about it, absorbing it, allowing the words and message to penetrate us.

It is also very useful to get two or three or more others together and to discuss a passage from Scripture as a group.